ENDORSEMENTS

"No matter how broken you feel, God is the great physician who can heal your broken heart."

—RICHARD PAUL EVANS
#1 *New York Times* bestselling author

"*Heartbreak Is Not My Home* by Dejah Edwards is an insightfully written story of pain and purpose, tragedy and triumph, and most of all unconditional love. If you're looking for an encouraging and even life-changing story, this is the book for you. Highly recommended!"

—KATHI MACIAS, bestselling author
of more than 50 books. kathimacias.com

"Written with a heart of compassion, author Dejah Edwards crafts a story of not only one woman's search for unconditional love; she depicts a life desperate for second, third, and fourth chances. *Heartbreak Is Not My Home* follows Darla Greystone's early life and how it has been marked by poor decisions and pivotal life choices. Picking men—and trusting them—is one of them. A relationship with Jesse marks the beginning of a series of regrettable choices. Poor choices have consequences—and for Darla, an attractive and well-educated young woman, one of her choices leads to an unexpected pregnancy, an abortion, and the crushing weight of guilt and shame. She will later learn from a friend that only placing her faith in Jesus Christ can repair her brokenness and build a bridge to a better life. Now she must make another choice. A choice we all face. Will she choose to have her life defined by her faith—or her failures."

—JAMES C. MAGRUDER, author of *The Glimpse* and recently, the award-winning novel, *The Desert Between Us*

"A Powerful Journey of Heartache, Healing, and Hope. This beautifully written novel follows Darla Greystone's emotional journey in search of unconditional love. From youthful rebellion and heartbreak to devastating choices and betrayal, Darla's story is raw, honest, and deeply moving. The story is not only about finding love but also discovering purpose and peace in God's grace. The author provides a touching and inspiring read that will resonate with anyone who has ever searched for love, affection, and true meaning and found it when they gave their heart to Jesus."

—MARY GARDEN HUGHES, author of *The Last Slow Dance*, *The Gift of the Music Maker* and coming soon *Harry and Tess Were Married*

"From Innocence to deception to renewal, *Heartbreak Is Not My Home* weaves a beautiful story of hope and healing. Dejah Edwards is a master storyteller, once again capturing real-life emotions and struggles."

—PAM FRIOLI, author of *Journey of Secrets*

"*Heartbreak Is Not My Home* by Dejah Edwards will help to rebuild hope in anyone who feels they've lost it—especially in relationships that were either compromised or short-lived. The healing and restoration for any broken heart is truly a loving God, who will love us unconditionally and strengthen us on our journey through life's challenges."

—PASTORS ART & KUNA SEPULVEDA, Senior Pastors, Word of Life Christian Center, Honolulu, Hawaii

"Once again, Dejah Edwards has taken the reader from a world of pain, to a story of love and redemption. By carefully weaving the journey of Darla through the many devastating disappointments she experiences, the authors storytelling gift shines bright.

This is a must read for anyone searching for the treasure of a love only God can give."

—PASTOR TOM VILLALOBOS, Oak Valley Church, Yucaipa, California

HEARTBREAK
IS NOT MY
HOME

DEJAH EDWARDS

Deeply Loved By Him
BOOKS

For information contact:
dejah05@gmail.com
www.deeplylovedbyhim.com

Published by:
Deeply Loved By Him Books

All scripture references are taken from The Amplified Bible,
1954, 1958, 1962, 1964, 1965, 1987
By the Lockman Foundation
Used by permission.

Cover design by: Santo Roy
99designs.com/profiles/santoroy71

Interior book design by Francine Platt • Eden Graphics, Inc.
edengraphics.net

Paperback ISBN 978-1-960007-85-8
eBook ISBN 978-1-960007-86-5

Library of Congress Control Number: 2025916261

Manufactured in the United States of America
First Edition

I dedicate this book to the memory of my parents, Ruth and Anthony Bertone, whose lives painted a portrait of God's love for me —and awakened the belief that there are no bounds to what I can achieve—if only I believe.

ACKNOWLEDGMENTS

A SPECIAL THANKS to Richard Paul Evans for helping me so much to recognize my potential as a writer. And to those other writers who are part of our Author Ready tribe for your input, support, and encouragement.

To Ron, my husband and best friend, thank you seems inadequate. Without your patience, understanding, and willingness to let me sit for hours upon hours at the computer uninterrupted, I would not be able to fulfill my passion and purpose as a writer.

I would like to express my deepest appreciation to my pastor, Tom Villalobos, for sharing your idea for the theme of my book—broken hearts. It was the spark that ignited this story.

No book would be complete without the input and keen eyes of editors and beta readers. Thank you to my excellent editors, Joanna Harris and Kim Autrey, for helping me polish my words and organize my thoughts.

I am most grateful to my heavenly Father who inspired me to create a story of redemption and restoration to share with others. May this book glorify His name and proclaim His healing power.

He heals the brokenhearted and binds up their wounds (healing their pain and comforting their sorrow).

— PSALM 147:3 AMP

PROLOGUE

January 1973

"RELAX YOUNG LADY, your problem will soon be over."
My problem? This doctor is clueless.
The drug slowly took over. Darla's body drifted into euphoria.

MY PROBLEM? Her mind screamed. *It's not a problem. It's a baabby. It's murder. I'm a murderer.*

Blackness.

1

August 1969

Darla sat in a booth at Mr. G's Diner, a local coffee shop on Saturday morning. She was waiting for her friend Amy's shift to end. Amy worked there part-time for the summer.

Amy finally sat down and squealed, "Look out the window."

Darla grabbed onto her friend's arm. "Wow, that's a real hippie Volkswagen bus."

She stared at the lime green VW bus. A big black peace sign was painted on the side door.

"I've never seen anything like that here in Larchmont." Amy laughed at the people who walked by the bus and took a second look. "Darla, take a look at the guy getting out of the bus."

"Oh my! I love his long hair."

Out stepped a young man wearing a leather cowboy

hat, a tie-dyed blue shirt, and bell-bottom jeans. He slowly walked into the coffee shop and glanced around. The interesting stranger saw the two girls sitting at a table. Smiling, he came over to Darla and Amy. He removed his hat and bowed low.

"Hi, ladies. What's good to eat here?"

Darla answered right away. "My favorite is the double BLT. It comes with avocado. I usually get a cola or an egg cream to go with it."

"I think I'll order that. By the way, what's an egg cream?"

"It's a New York drink—no eggs—just milk, chocolate syrup, and seltzer water."

"Would you like to join us? I see your license plate says Massachusetts. So obviously you're not from around here and don't know anyone," asked Amy.

"I'm from Stockbridge, Massachusetts—the home of Alice's Restaurant."

"You mean the song by Arlo Guthrie," Darla blurted out, obviously impressed. "My name is Darla, and this is my best friend, Amy."

"Glad to meet you groovy ladies. I'm Tyler."

The waitress came over and took Tyler's order. The girls ordered refills of their sodas.

"How cool." Amy smiled. "I adore Arlo."

"Me too. That's why I'm here. I'm picking up my cousin and his lady in Katonah. We're meeting up with my girlfriend. She's driving in from Connecticut with some friends. Then we're headed to Woodstock to see Arlo live."

Darla looked over at Amy. Amy shrugged her shoulders.

Together the girls asked, "What's Woodstock?"

"It's a three-day music and art festival. Thirty-two musicians are expected to perform there. People like Jefferson Airplane, Janis Joplin, Jimi Hendrix. It's going to be outside on this guy Max Yasgur's dairy farm. A thousand people are expected to be there. I have an artist pass I purchased along with my ticket so I can get right in. Hey, you ladies want to come? I have the room and some extra tickets. I'm going to my cousin's today. We plan to leave on Monday. We want to get there early to get a good spot close to the stage to set up my art work. I could stop back by and pick you up."

Amy looked sad. "I can't go. Unfortunately, I have to work."

"I'll go," Darla almost shouted. "I have nothing to do until graduate school starts in September. This sounds so cool."

Amy stared at her in disbelief.

"Groovy. How about you meet me here at 9:00 a.m. Monday? We're bringing the water and food. Just pack your clothes."

Darla said good-bye to Tyler. He got up to leave and hugged both girls.

Before he walked out the door, he turned around. "See you Monday, Darla."

Amy narrowed her eyes. She looked at Darla like she was crazy.

Darla thought of Woodstock as a time to break away and have fun. She was unaware the one decision she would make today would alter the course of her life forever.

"Why did you tell Tyler you would go?"

"Because I am."

"Your parents will never let you go."

"They don't have to know. My life's been planned out for me. My parents try to mold me into what they want me to be. I feel as if I have no freedom to choose."

"What are you saying? You have everything you could ever want. You've grown up in affluence—your dad is a successful neurosurgeon, and your mother is quite the socialite. You're loaded with talent and beauty. You were the most popular girl in high school and the smartest. You were selected to attend Sarah Lawrence College with an SAT score of 1550."

"Yes, Amy, but that's where my mother went to college. I have always had to live up to their standards."

"What do you mean they don't have to know?"

"Did you forget? They leave tomorrow for a ten day cruise to Cancun. I'll tell them I don't want to stay home with my brother. Instead, I prefer to stay at your house."

"Oh no. Don't put me in the middle of that."

"Amy, we've been friends since elementary school when your mom enrolled you in my dance class. I've always envied you. When I went to your house, your mom made it warm and inviting. My house feels cold and resembles a model home. Your mother made cookies with us and let you have a dog. My mom said dogs were dirty and only once asked the housekeeper to make cookies with me. My parents are good to me, but I often feel neglected. My mom's more busy with society lunches at the country club than spending time with me."

"I know what you mean, Darla. Your parents are definitely members of the elite in our wealthy town of Larchmont.

My mom can only afford to live here on her nurse's salary because she acquired our house in the divorce settlement. I still don't want to be blamed for your rebellion."

"You won't be. They'll never know. If they ever find out, I'll say you knew nothing about it."

"Actually, Larchmont is an idyllic community—a desirable place to live—safe neighborhoods, great schools, and a walkable downtown. I want to see more. I want some adventure on my own."

"Oh, all right." Amy finally gave in. "Actually, I'm jealous. I wish I could go. It sounds like it's going to be so cool." Amy frowned, shaking her head. "At least I'd fit in easily with my thrift store clothes. Darla, you can't wear your designer clothes to a rock concert. You'll stand out like a sore thumb. On your way home, why don't you run over to the thrift store and get some jeans. Cut them off for short shorts."

"You're right. I want to fit in. I don't want to look like some rich kid from Larchmont."

Although my life seemed perfect to everyone else, I've felt stifled. My mother named me Darla after Our Gang Comedy *TV show because she wanted to push me into the theatre and dancing. Her influence got me the role of* Little Miss Sunshine *at the community theatre. I want to be liked for who I am not because of who my parents are or where I've grown up.*

At the thrift store, Darla found just what she needed: two pairs of faded jeans in her size. On one of the jeans someone had sewed rhinestones along the pockets. Her best find was a purple tie-dyed tank top and a hot pink one. She also purchased a light blue hooded sweatshirt and a pair of leather Birkenstock sandals.

Darla stopped at Amy's house to show her treasures to her friend. Amy was busy ordering a pizza. Darla wished she could stay. She loved eating over at her friend's house. Amy's mom often fixed mac and cheese or tacos. Darla never had those things at her house—too many carbs, unhealthy.

"You did good, Darla. I love the tie-dyed purple top. The hot pink will look great with your tan. I have a canvas backpack you can borrow."

"Thanks so much. I better get home. We're having a family dinner together before my parents leave tomorrow. I don't want them to get suspicious."

"Give me the things you got at the thrift store. I'll wash them, cut off the jeans, and pack them for you. My mom will be at work until late tonight. I won't have to explain anything to her."

"I love you, Amy. You're the best."

Amy always comes through for me. I couldn't ask for a better friend. She understands me and knows I need to break free and do this for myself.

2

DURING DINNER THAT NIGHT, Darla tried to relax and make small talk even though she was bursting with excitement about going to Woodstock. She didn't want anyone to suspect anything out of the ordinary.

"Hey, Mom. Is it okay if I spend a few nights at Amy's while your gone? She has some days off, and we wanted to hang out."

"Sure, dear. I'm sure you'll have more fun with your best friend than staying home with your brother."

Darla tried hard to hide her delight. She had pulled it off.

"Can I have another piece of pie?" she asked with a smile.

"Of course."

Darla couldn't fall asleep that night. Excitement. Anticipation. Freedom.

I am finally doing something I want to do—not something someone else chose for me. All my life they chose specific private schools, mandated participation in theatre and dance and forced their lifestyle on me. I was taught to comply without questioning.

The next day, her parents left for vacation. She hugged them and wished them a wonderful time.

Once they were gone, she hurried to the Woolworth's store. She planned to buy some beads to put in her hair. When she got home, Amy phoned.

"Listen, I only had to work the morning shift. Why don't you come over, bring the rest of the stuff you're taking with you and spend the night."

"Cool. I bought different colored beads. You can help me experiment putting them in my hair."

Darla hurried and packed several pairs of underwear, toiletries, and makeup. On her way out, she grabbed some packages of peanut butter snacks and granola bars. She left a note for her brother and walked over to Amy's house.

Amy met her at the door. "Look what I found." She held up a magazine. "There's an article with instructions on how to weave beads into your hair."

"Let's do it."

Darla and Amy practiced until they got it right, talking as they worked. Saffron, Amy's golden retriever, sat on the bed next to Darla. Darla stroked her head.

"Amy, someday I'm going to have a dog. I hate that my mother cares more about how the house looks than us having a pet. You are so lucky you got to work part-time at a veterinarian hospital during high school. That's what made you want to go to Cornell University for veterinary medicine. In September, you'll get to do what you always dreamed of—be a vet. I hope I am as certain as you are of my career choice when I finish my masters in Psychology."

"You'll do fine. You have excelled in everything since I've known you."

"I think it looks awesome in your strawberry blonde hair," Amy said. "Look the beads bring out your blue/green eyes. We should have no problem doing this again, Darla."

"Okay, Amy. I'll wash my hair tonight. We'll get up early and style it with the beads."

The next morning, after Amy fixed Darla's hair in beaded braids, Amy's mom made them French toast. When they finished eating, both girls rushed over to the coffee shop.

Amy wasn't scheduled to work until 10:00 a.m. She was curious to see Tyler's cousin. The Volkswagen bus pulled up minutes after the girls arrived. Tyler and three other people jumped out. Tyler wore bell bottoms again with a t-shirt saying Make Love Not War.

"Hi, ladies. This is my cousin Eddie and his girlfriend Summer, and my girlfriend Lacy."

Eddie put up his fingers showing a peace sign. His blond hair hung to his shoulders. He wore a denim shirt with jeans. Round, rose-colored glasses adorned his face. Summer nodded her head and smiled. She was petite with dark brown, spiral perm curly hair that cascaded down her back.

Her eyes were amber colored with an upturned nose and a cute smile. She wore cutoff jeans and an embroidered peasant blouse. Multiple bracelets layered her wrists. Lacy smiled. Her cute face was covered with freckles. A flower headband decorated her braided red hair. She wore a bright long floral dress and white moccasins.

Tyler took Darla's backpack and put it in the back of the VW.

"You can ride shotgun with me and Lacy, Darla. Summer and Eddie want to ride in the back so they can work on their jewelry."

Amy hugged Darla. "Have fun! I can't wait to hear all about it."

"I will. Bye." Darla hopped in the bus. They took off down the road. Tyler put in an eight-track tape. Arlo's voice rang out. They all sang along. For the first time in her life, Darla felt free.

Once they got way out in the county, Eddie held up a joint. "Hey, cuz, I only brought one just in case we got stopped. You know with you driving this VW bus with out-of-state tags and a peace sign."

"Far out. Light it up, man."

Darla never smoked pot before. Actually, she never smoked anything.

Well, why not. I want to have a good time.

When they passed the joint to her, she coughed a lot.

"Inhale it slow like this." Eddie showed her.

It didn't take much for Darla to get high. The next thing she knew, she was hungry. Summer passed around some red and black licorice. Darla thought licorice never tasted this good.

"We must be getting close. Look at all these cars on the road."

"You're right, Tyler. It takes about two hours to Bethel from Larchmont. We've been on the road about an hour and a half."

The traffic ahead moved slowly. Finally, they saw the sign—Woodstock Music and Art Festival.

3

AFTER TYLER PARKED THE BUS, Darla said, "Wow, so cool, you had the artist pass. We got right in the separate entrance and didn't have to wait in that line."

They got out and stretched their legs. Eddie took out a little camping stove and grilled hot dogs. Summer and Darla got out the lawn chairs, a few bags of chips, and soda. Summer reached into one of the boxes she took out of the bus.

"Here, Darla. This is for you. It matches your eyes." Darla put on the greenish blue beaded bracelet.

"Thank you so much. I love it."

"The bead in the middle is called the beaming sun. It's actually a gemstone that is linked to the sun and was thought to have magical properties. People believed if you rubbed this stone, you would find love."

Darla smiled and gave Summer a big hug. The other venders were busy setting up their handmade items. After helping Tyler, Lacy, Summer, and Eddie set up their goods for sale, Darla noticed a large group of people gathering not far away. She walked over and saw a guy standing in the middle of the crowd. Stepping closer she heard him explaining Kundalini yoga.

"If you are interested in joining us in a practice, I will lead you."

Darla joined the yoga group. She learned breathing techniques that would free up stuck energy and enhance energy levels. She felt euphoric when the practice ended.

She ran back to her friends to let them know how wonderful the yoga made her feel. Tyler and Eddie were busy cooking veggie burgers and beans. Summer was making more bracelets.

After they ate, Tyler took out his guitar and sang. He sure could sing. Soon others came over and joined in. Someone brought a few bottles of wine. They passed the wine around. The group partied well into the night. One by one, they climbed into the bus and fell asleep.

The next morning, when the guys went to find a restroom, Summer helped Darla fix her hair.

When the guys returned, they pointed the way to the facilities. The line wasn't as bad as Darla thought it would be. It was her first time using a porta potty.

When they returned, Summer brought some clothes out on a rack to sell. Darla spotted a powder blue peasant top like the one Summer wore yesterday. She handed Summer a twenty dollar bill.

"I'll take this one."

"Thanks, you're my first sale of the day."

Darla went in the bus and changed into the top.

"It looks terrific on you."

"Cool." Darla laughed and grabbed a water bottle. "I think I'll go explore."

"Don't get lost. The bands are arriving. They are setting up today. You may run into Arlo." Tyler winked.

"Far out," said Eddie

As Darla walked around, she felt as if she'd been transported into a new world. Everyone smiled. Everyone said Hi.

Last night all the kids who joined our group acted like we'd known them forever. They were friendly and generous. No one looked down on anyone. We were all equal. This is peace.

Her thoughts suddenly were interrupted by a friendly voice. Darla looked all around.

"I'm down here. Hi. Would you like to share my blanket?"

Darla sat down and looked over at the boy wearing a UCLA t-shirt and jeans cut off just above his knees. On his feet were leather Birkenstock sandals. A leather ankle bracelet was on his leg and a beaded leather bracelet on his wrist.

"Sure."

He moved closer to Darla, and she looked into the face of someone who could have been cast in the knights of the roundtable. His shoulder-length brown hair was cut into an almost Dutch boy haircut. The brown hair streaked with gold—Darla assumed, noting his t-shirt—was kissed by the sun. His big puppy dog eyes gave him a look of unsophisticated innocence. His smile was warm and inviting like a long awaited summer breeze.

"Hi. My name is Jesse."

"I'm Darla."

"Like Darla from *Our Gang?*"

"The same."

"I see the resemblance. You are much cuter." Jesse smiled again. Darla blushed.

"Where are you from, Darla?"

"Larchmont, New York."

"Where's that?"

"About two hours from here. It's a peaceful seaside village in the town of Mamaroneck. A very desirable place to live—commuter-friendly because of its close proximity to Manhattan."

"And you?"

"California."

"Wow, that's a long way. I've always wanted to go to California."

"Yeah, my brother and I made it a road trip. We left two weeks ago and made several site seeing stops along the way."

"Sounds cool."

"It was. We had to come to Woodstock. All these great musicians in one place. The Who, Janis Joplin, Jefferson Airplane, Jimi Hendrix, Arlo Guthrie, and more. I think this festival will make history. All these kids getting along. Peace and love. The spirit of Woodstock. I want to be part of it."

"Me too. That's why I'm here." Darla's eyes sparkled as she hung on to every word Jesse spoke.

Wow he really seems interested in me.

"So you go to UCLA? What's your major?"

"Biology. I want to go into medical research. And you, Darla, you go to college?"

"I just graduated in May."

"What school?"

"Sarah Lawrence."

"Wow, rich girl. Isn't that just for girls?"

"It was. It changed to co-ed last year. So preppy boys and snobby girls." Darla shrugged.

"You don't look like a snob. You seem like a sweet young lady. What was your major?"

"Psychology. My parents wanted me go into medicine—like my father and brother. I don't like blood so instead, they settled on Psychology."

"You want to get into people's heads?"

"I'm starting graduate school at Sarah Lawrence next month to get my masters in behavioral psychology and do counseling."

"Tell me, pretty lady, why did you come to Woodstock?"

"When Tyler, the artist guy who drove us up here, told me about it, I knew I had to come. Aside from the great music, it was something I decided to do for myself. No one chose for me. You see, my whole life has been planned out for me, since I was a little girl. No risks. No adventures. So here I am."

"I can dig it. Well, my dear, I'd like to help you enjoy your adventure."

Jesse took Darla by the hand.

"Come on. I want you to meet my brother and his lady. He's setting up some tents over there."

Darla gasped. Her eyebrows rose and her mouth gaped open. Her eyes shifted back and forth to the boy standing there back to Jesse.

"Yes. We're twins. He's eleven minutes older. Darla, this is Jamie."

"Hi, Darla—from *Our Gang?*"

Everyone laughed. Just then a tall, slim girl wearing a denim, flowered dress walked up.

"Darla, this is Autumn. She's my lady," Jamie said.

Autumn reminded Darla of a fairy with her black pixie haircut and her big, soft eyes. "Hey, isn't this groovy?" Jamie put his arm around Autumn.

"Thanks for setting up the tents. Darla and I are going to walk around some." Jesse took Darla's hand once more. She looked up at him and smiled.

"Come. I want to introduce you to the people I came with," Darla said.

4

SUMMER WINKED AT DARLA when they showed up. After
introductions were made, Jesse asked Tyler if he could
see his guitar. Jesse sat down, strummed the guitar, and sang
a song they all knew "Sugar, Sugar."

Darla leaned forward as her eyes widened. She had no
idea he could sing like that.

"Wow, man. You're really good," commented Tyler.

Summer nodded her head and grinned at Darla. "Play
some more. I'm going to make some peanut butter and jelly
sandwiches. Eddie, get the wine coolers out of the bus."

Jesse sang a love song by the Beatles "Something." They
enjoyed the sandwiches and the wine.

Jesse looked at Darla. "Let's get back up to our spot. I
think they might start the music tonight."

He helped her up. "See you all later."

"Have fun," Lacy shouted after them. Darla was surprised to find that Jesse's blanket was still in the same spot
where they left it.

About fifty people had gathered nearby. When Darla

and Jesse sat, someone passed around a bottle of wine and a joint. Jesse indulged.

Darla let it pass by her.

Jesse looked intently at Darla. "Look at all this peace and love—everyone's getting along—no anger—no fights—no prejudice. As far as you can see people. Thousands of people just loving one another. Sharing. Caring. Why can't the world be like that? Why are we fighting a senseless war. Killing people. My brother, just out of high school, got drafted. Never was out of California. He came home in a body bag. It's all senseless."

Tears welled up in Darla's eyes. *His brother. Oh no.* She took Jesse by the hand.

"I am sorry. So sorry." She had never thought about the things Jesse talked about. She lived secure and safe in her little community. Immediately, Darla felt selfish and regretful.

The world is falling apart. I'm just going on with life like nothing's wrong.

It started to pour rain. Jesse rushed her over to his tent.

"Here's one of my shirts. Get out of your top. You're dripping wet. I don't want you to catch a cold."

Darla turned around and slipped on his shirt. He hung both their shirts up in the tent to dry. Jesse picked up his guitar and sang. Darla's heart melted. He sang a love song to her "Crimson and Clover."

"Here, try one of these." Jesse handed her a brownie. "Only eat half. They're pretty potent."

Darla broke the brownie in half. She ate it and gave the other half to Jesse. It didn't take long for Darla to feel the effects of the brownie. Jesse sang. Darla smiled. Soon they both started laughing about everything. The rain pounded on the tent. They peeked out only to see people scrambling all over for shelter.

Darla didn't know when she fell asleep. She woke up in Jesse's arms.

"Hey, you guys," Jamie yelled from outside the tent. "We found some makeshift showers. You need to hurry. The music is scheduled to start soon."

Darla grabbed her top. It was almost completely dry. Jesse helped her up. He grabbed some shampoo and body wash. Darla carefully removed the beads from her hair.

"Wow. It will feel good to wash."

"Sure will."

They hurried after Jamie and Autumn. The crowd at the showers was still relatively small. After they finished cleaning up, Jamie took them over to the Hog Farm—a group passing out healthy food—bran muffins, bananas, and juice.

The sun shone brightly. Jesse hung their wet towels over the tent and grabbed a dry blanket.

Darla combed her hair.

"Leave your hair down today. It looks groovy."

"Okay."

Jamie came over with Autumn. They sat down with Darla and Jesse. He took some brownies out of his pocket. He handed them out.

"Only give Darla half. It's too strong for her."

"Right."

Chip Monck, the stage manager, announced, "This is

now a free concert. There are over four hundred thousand people gathered here. That doesn't mean anything goes. But what that means is we're going to put the music up for free. The people backing the festival are going to get hurt. What these people have in their heads is that your welfare and the music is a lot more important than a dollar. Let's welcome Richie Havens."

The music rang out. Everyone got up dancing along with the beat. Richie Havens sang the song "Freedom."

Darla thought the lyrics to that song were perfect for her right at the moment. She never felt this free before or this far from her home. He sang for three hours. Jesse motioned for Darla to sit down. He handed Darla a rice cake with peanut butter and jelly and a bottled water.

Darla smacked her lips. *Peanut butter never tasted this good.*

The weather turned muggy and hot. Both Jesse and Jamie no longer wore their shirts. Autumn wore a bathing suit top with short shorts.

"Hey, Darla, I have another bathing suit top that may fit you."

Darla followed Autumn to their tent. The denim bathing suit top fit except the cup size could have been a little larger.

"What do you think, Autumn?"

"I think it definitely accentuates your figure. Actually, I lost the bottoms to it. So go ahead and keep the top. You fill it out better than I do."

When the girls returned, Jesse's eyebrow went up. "You sure are wearing that top."

Darla blushed. Jesse winked at her and put his arm around her and drew her close. The music played well into the night. Jamie's brownies kept them high.

Hugging herself with delight, she felt a part of every song. Her body swayed along with the music. *Is this what freedom feels like?*

∽ 5 ∽

WHEN ARLO GUTHRIE appeared on stage, Jesse and Jamie went wild, jumping up and down. After Arlo finished singing "Coming into Los Angeles," he stopped and addressed the crowd.

"Man, this is far out," Arlo shouted. "This is the largest city in New York. The mayor, Nelson Rockefeller, declared Sullivan County a state of emergency."

This must be because they didn't expect this many people. They must be worried about enough food. I bet there's traffic jams.

During the next performance by Joan Baez, it started to drizzle.

"Come on, Darla. Let's hurry back to the tent. It's about to pour."

Jamie and Autumn followed behind. Before going into his tent. Jamie handed Jesse a fat joint.

"Enjoy, bro."

In the tent, Jesse lit up and took a long drag. Then he handed it to Darla. She hesitated at first, then thought, *Why not. I'm out to have fun. I feel safe with Jesse.*

Before they finished the joint, Darla announced, "I need to use the restroom."

"Here, take my hand." Jesse grabbed a flashlight and led her outside. They walked to the porta potty. It was still only drizzling.

On the way back, someone stopped Jesse. "Hey, man, we have some extra cold drinks. Want some?"

"Sure, thanks."

Jesse took two cans and handed one to Darla. The cold soda tasted refreshing after the muggy, hot day.

When they got to the tent, Darla asked Jesse, "Is there any ice left in the cooler?"

"Yes."

He handed her some ice, and she wrapped it in a towel and rubbed it on her face, arms, and legs.

Jesse lit the joint back up and handed it to her after he took a long drag.

"Here, let me help you." He took the towel from her. He started rubbing it down her back.

"That feels great."

"I bet this would feel even better."

He slowly untied her bathing suit top. He grabbled some more ice and wrapped it in the towel. Gently, he brought it around to her front. Tenderly, he stroked her. All her inhibitions faded, she stared into his face as he laid her down. Darla closed her eyes. The world disappeared. It was their moment. Their time. It felt wonderful to become one with Jesse.

Darla awakened to music and Jamie shouting, "Hey, you two sleepy heads, the music's already started. We need to go get some breakfast before its all gone."

Jesse and Darla quickly got themselves together and stepped outside. The sky was overcast and cooler than it was yesterday.

Darla and Autumn got in line for the shower. Jesse and Jamie went to get some food.

The boys returned. "Look who we ran into at the Hog Farm." There stood Tyler, Eddie, and Summer. They all hugged. Then Jesse and Jaime jumped into the shower.

Tyler spoke to Darla. "We are staying until Monday morning. No sense in trying to leave. The roads are jammed."

"All right. I'll meet you at the bus after the last act."

"Sounds good. Have fun. Stay safe."

Summer came over to Darla. "It looks like Jesse really digs you. He's so cute. Hold on to that one."

Darla smiled. "I plan to."

Jesse and Jamie returned to the group. Jessie took Darla by the hand.

"See you guys later."

The four of them sat down in front of the stage. Jamie took out the granola bars and apples he got at the Hog Farm. The music played on all day. Darla reminisced about the words Melanie sang in her song "Beautiful People." She thought about the people here at Woodstock and how she would never have noticed them a week ago. Now she looked at people differently.

She must have dozed off. Jesse shook her. Blinking, she opened her eyes.

"Darla, have you ever heard anyone play guitar like that? He's the best."

Darla sat up, just as Jimi Hendrix blurted out "The Star Spangled Banner" on his guitar. Kids all around stood in a patriotic stance honoring their country. Truly an emotional moment. Tears fell down her cheeks. The war in Vietnam, the hatred for those in another country, the prejudice, all the fear and turmoil of the day weighed heavy on her heart. Woodstock to her was a release from all of it.

The '60s was definitely a time of unrest. The kids at Woodstock found a few days to escape and find peace. Would this peace last?

For Darla, being at Woodstock was almost a religious experience. Her parents rarely attended church—Easter and Christmas only. Her dad played golf on Sundays. When her grandmother was alive, she took Darla to church. Darla remembered the big Bible on her grandmother's coffee table. Sometimes she would read to Darla from it. That was a long time ago. Darla believed there was a God but never thought too much about it.

It was a time to break free, reflect, and reassess her life path. Something changed in her. She knew she didn't want to follow after her parents' values. Money, country clubs, and social status didn't matter to her as an independent woman. Making a difference in the world did. Vietnam was never on her mind. Many of the young men in her quaint little town of Larchmont were exempt from the draft. They went right from high school to college. Such was the case with her brother. Now she saw things differently. Her heart ached for the young boys who fought in a country they knew nothing about, only to return home in a body bag. What about the innocent civilians losing their loved ones and homes in Vietnam. Jesse cared about these things. Many times in the last few days, he shared with her his opposition to the war. Friends of his had burned their draft cards and moved to Canada. Darla returned to the moment. Hendrix still played "The Star Spangled Banner."

Looking around, thousands of kids still continued to stand in respect for the United States. Her heart was overwhelmed with the reality that she lived in the freest country on earth. She glanced over at Jesse, and there were tears in his eyes, his hand over his heart. It seemed appropriate that the grand finale would include this song.

When Jimi Hendrix finished, Jesse pulled Darla to her feet.

"Look, half the crowd's left. I need to get you to your friends who are taking you home."

Everything moved too fast. When they arrived at Tyler's bus, they already were loaded up. Jesse and Darla quickly exchanged phone numbers and addresses. He hugged her close. Looked into her eyes. "You'll see me again. That's a promise."

Darla's mouth gaped open. There was so much she wanted to say. They were out of time. Jesse turned to leave. Darla stood watching him walk away.

She jumped into the bus.

Summer tried to console her. "He seems to really dig you. He asked for your contact information first. Don't lose hope."

Was all this real or was it just part of the magic of Woodstock?

6

Darla slept most of the way home. She was glad no one was home when she arrived, dirty and exhausted. She didn't have to explain her condition to anyone. Her parents weren't due back until the weekend. She had plenty of time to recover.

Standing in the hot shower, she could still feel Jesse's touch. After the shower, she took all her dirty clothes to the laundry room. Emptying her pockets she found a folded up paper. In it was a picture of Jesse, the leather bracelet he wore on his wrist, and a note that read:

You are the coolest girl I ever met. Thanks for being with me. I'll never forget you. Love, Jesse

Does he really mean that? Does he really see me as unforgettable? Darla longed for Jesse. A tear slid down her cheek. *All I'm desiring is to be loved for who I am—not because of who my parents are and what they have.*

Startled by the ring of the phone, she wiped her eye and answered the phone. Amy's voice greeted her. "Wow, you're back. I want to hear all about it. I watched clips of the festival on the news. It sure looked cool. Can you meet me at Mr. G's café?"

"Sure, Amy. I just hoped out of the shower. Be there in thirty minutes."

When Darla arrived at G's café, Amy ran over and hugged her. Then she stepped back.

"What happened to you? You're glowing."

Just as Darla started to respond, Amy's eyes grew big.

"Will you look at him. Where did he come from?"

Darla looked up and froze. She and Jesse's eyes locked. A huge smile spread over Jesse's face.

He slowly walked over to her.

"Jesse, what are you doing here?"

"I couldn't stay away. I had to see you again."

"But how did you know I was here?" Darla asked.

"I phoned your house. I guess it was your brother who gave me this address. He said you'd probably be meeting your friend here."

Amy sat with her mouth open.

"I take it this is your friend?" Jesse said.

"Yes. Jesse, meet my oldest and dearest friend, Amy."

"Glad to meet you."

Just then Jaime and Autumn walked in. Jesse waved them over.

After introductions, Jesse said, "I wanted to see where my girl lived before we headed back to California. Will you give me a tour of your town?"

"Sure."

"Autumn and I are going back to the motel. We want to

get some more rest before the long drive tomorrow," Jamie said as he started to walk away.

Jesse and Darla said good-bye to them and Amy, and then they walked around Larchmont.

"With its tree-lined streets, our little village has a small town charm," said Darla. "Living by the Long Island Sound, I grew up playing on the rocks on the shoreline. The neighborhoods are so safe. I could ride my bike all over town unsupervised."

"I see. Let's stop and get some ice cream."

Jesse ordered a mint chocolate chip cone with sprinkles and Darla got a coffee cone with sprinkles too. They sat at a small bistro table. Jesse glanced at Darla, his lips covered with ice cream dotting the biggest grin. She noticed how one curly lock of his hair fell aimlessly over his forehead. It was one of the first things she noticed about him—it added to his cuteness. Darla returned his smile. He gently took her hand.

"I'm so glad we stopped here on our way back to California. I feel like I know more about you now. I noticed when we were looking for the café, we passed an old time photo studio. Let's go there and take a picture together."

"Sure."

"Cool. Let's go for it."

They finished their ice cream and walked over to the photo shop. Jesse dressed up as a gunslinger complete with a cowboy hat and six shooters. Darla chose a blue satin dance hall dress. The photographer helped her pin up her hair the way women wore it during that era. She also used a curling iron to put Darla's hair in some curls that hung down her cheeks. Darla applied some stage makeup to enhance the photos. Jesse whooped when she appeared from the dressing room. The photographer positioned Darla siting on the bar and Jesse leaning into her.

"You two make such a darling couple," the photographer said. "Have you been together for a long time?"

"No, actually, we just met. But I don't plan to let her get away." Jesse winked at Darla.

"I'll have the photos ready for you in a couple of hours," the photographer told them.

"Thank you so much," Darla said. "I'll come back later to pick them up.

When they exited the shop, Jesse turned to her. "We're leaving very early in the morning. I'd like to take you out to dinner at the best restaurant in town."

"That would be Nick's On the Water in Mamaroneck."

Darla turned and hugged Jesse. He returned her hug with a tender kiss.

"How about we both go change into something more fancy. I'll pick you up at 5:30. Can you make reservations for us at 6:00?"

"Sounds great." She quickly gave him her address.

Darla floated home immersed in the thought of Jesse. *Oh my. What will I wear?* She soaked in a lavender oil bath for one hour. Then washed and styled her hair. She decided on a pale blue spaghetti strap dress with low black heels. On her ears she wore gold hoop earrings and her gold cross necklace her grandmother gave her before she passed away. Carefully, she applied her eye and face makeup to make it look more dramatic. For a finishing touch, she sprayed herself with Guerlain Chamade perfume. Taking a long look at herself in her full length mirror, she decided she never looked so elegant. When she went downstairs to wait for Jesse, her brother David remarked, "This guy must be really something. I've never seen you put in so much effort for a date."

Darla giggled.

"You look amazing for my little sister."

Just then the doorbell rang. David went to the door.

"Hi. I'm Jesse here to pick up Darla. You must be her brother."

"Glad to meet you. Yes, I'm David." He extended his hand to Jesse.

As they were shaking hands, Darla walked into the hall.

"Wow, you look gorgeous." Jesse whistled.

She noticed Jesse's clothes looked new. His jeans still had the pleats in them, and his denim shirt looked as if it just came off the rack.

"You look pretty handsome yourself."

Jesse took Darla's arm.

"You guys have fun," David called after them.

After they got into the car, Jesse hugged her. "You not only look stunning tonight, but you smell wonderful."

"After the way we smelled at Woodstock, I'm sure anything is an improvement." Darla giggled.

"After I left you this afternoon, I stopped into a store and bought some new clothes. I think the clothes I brought to Woodstock still smell like mud even after they were washed."

Darla had made the reservation at Nicks like she promised.

They were seated immediately by the window looking out at the water. A perfect view of the sunset.

Darla took out the photos she had picked up and handed one to Jesse. "We really look good together, Darla."

They both giggled.

Jesse took the lead and ordered for them. Two glasses of white Zinfandel, two Caesar salads, the surf and turf dinner which consisted of filet mignon and lobster tails. A vegetable medley of broccoli and cauliflower accompanied the meal.

While they awaited their meals, Jesse put a black velvet box in front of Darla.

"What's this?"

"Something special for you so you don't forget me." His eyes twinkled as he grinned at her.

Darla opened the box. She slapped her hands against her cheeks. "Oh my, I love it."

She gently removed the delicate gold bracelet. Hearts adorned the bracelet, appearing every quarter inch.

"Here, let me put it on you."

Darla lifted her left hand and Jesse fastened the clasp. She leaned over and kissed Jesse.

"Thank you."

The waiter delivered their wine and salads. Jesse lifted his glass.

"Let's toast. To the beautiful girl I found who I'm not going to let get away."

Darla felt warm all over. It wasn't just the wine. But the feelings awakening in her following Jesse's toast. She smiled and looked directly into his eyes.

Putting her hand on his, she whispered, "I don't want you to get away either. Let's enjoy right now."

For dessert, they split New York cheesecake topped with blueberries. Jesse paid the check. He took Darla by the hand and they walked down by the water. For a long time, they sat quietly on a bench. Jesse's arm around Darla and her head on his chest. Darla's eyes were closed.

"I wish time could stand still."

Jesse broke the silence.

"Whenever I gaze at the night sky or listen to the stillness of the ocean, I will think of this moment and remember you."

Darla nestled in closer. Their bodies melted together in a series of passionate kisses. Jesse pulled away first.

"I probably should get you home. Jamie wants to leave before sun up tomorrow. I need to get some rest. I'm sharing the driving with him."

They arrived at Darla's house and she clung to him. She kissed him with her whole being. When they came up for air, Jesse placed his hands on her cheeks, staring into her eyes.

"I have never felt like this before. Maybe this is what love looks like. It's tearing me apart to have to leave you. I need to figure out a way to get you to California."

"I can't imagine being away from you either. My master's program is for two years."

"I want to steal you away from here and take you home with me."

"I know, Jesse, and I'd gladly go. Let's just wait and see

what happens with time and separation. I do think I love you."

Jesse hugged her tight. He opened his door, walked around the car, and helped her out. Slowly they strolled to her front door

With one final kiss, Jesse said, "Please don't forget me."

"There's no way I ever could."

He turned around and got back in the car. The car pulled away. Darla stood for a long time looking after him.

Later that night, lying in bed, she still felt his embrace and tasted his lips.

Three days later, Darla's parents returned. Immediately, they noticed a change in their daughter. She seemed more reserved yet determined. Instead of living for the next party, pizza, or shopping spree, she genuinely showed concern over the war in Vietnam and the controversy surrounding it. She openly took an intelligent stand on her beliefs. Her parents expressed shock when she boarded a bus with other young people to protest in Washington, DC. She arrived home with a heavy heart after learning of all the young boys who had sacrificed their lives over a conflict she never thought we should be in.

Where is God in all this? If there is a God, why does he allow all this suffering and killing?

7

September 1969

GRADUATE SCHOOL STARTED. Darla threw herself into her studies. She wanted to be the best counselor she could be.

"I want to help people. I think this is a meaningful career. It can allow me to connect with others and help them through some of the most difficult and challenging moments of their lives," Darla declared one night to her parents.

Darla's mother rolled her eyes. "Of course we are proud of you and your efforts. What about your social life? You don't seem to make time for fun or your friends anymore."

"There's plenty of time for that after I get my degree."

Her parents looked at one another and shrugged their shoulders.

"Are you even dating someone at school? You need to go out and meet people."

"Oh mother, leave me alone. You have pressured me all my life to excel in school. That's what I'm trying to do. Graduate school is much more work than undergraduate." Darla ran to her room and slammed the door.

Why won't they leave me alone. They're always trying to run my life. Why do I have a need to meet their expectations or standards in order to feel sure of their love and support. It's not okay for me to be myself—I need to live up to an impossible ideal to deserve their love.

Darla flung herself on her bed. She grabbed the picture of her and Jesse.

Oh, Jesse, my love, you're the only one who loves me unconditionally.

Her parents didn't stop pushing. A month later when Darla came home from school, Darla's mother had prepared a special dinner party. One of her dad's fellow doctors and his wife were invited. Darla's mouth dropped when they walked in with their son who was doing his residency at her father's hospital.

"Darla, you remember the Wilsons. This is their son, Tad, he just finished medical school."

Darla managed a fake smile and a cordial greeting. She glanced over at her mother with cold, hard eyes. Her mother, looking proud, didn't even get Darla's message. During the meal, Darla's parents did all they could to engage her in conversation with Tad.

Finally, her mother spoke up, "Why don't you young people go get some ice cream. You're probably bored with us old folks."

Darla wanted to hide as she squeezed her eyes shut.

This is it. They've gone too far this time.

Before she knew what was happening, Tad was pulling her chair out for her. "Come on, Darla. It's a nice night. Let's take a walk."

Reluctantly, she followed him. She just wanted to get away from her parents.

Tad spoke first, "I'm so sorry for that. My parents are always trying to fix me up too. I have a girlfriend I met when I was away at college. She's a daycare teacher. I'm afraid she wouldn't fit into my parents' social status. I'm at the point that I don't care. I don't want to be like them."

"I know what you mean," Darla said. "I have a boyfriend in California. It's always been one of my dreams to go out to California. When I graduate, I want to move out there—away from this."

Darla waited until the Wilson's left before she stormed into the house.

"How dare you humiliate me like that? Stay out of my life."

"But dear, we were only trying to help," her mother pleaded.

"Stop. I don't need your help." Once again, Darla retreated to the sanctity of her room.

Jesse continued communicating with Darla. He phoned her at least once a week. Their conversations usually centered around school, Jaime, and Amy. She received cute cards from him regularly. He often enclosed pictures of himself surfing or just hanging out with Jamie. At Christmas, he sent a throw blanket with a scene from Yosemite National Park. The note enclosed in it read: *I'll take you here one day, Love, Jesse.* All of his cards and phone calls ended the same: *I've never met anyone like you. Soon you'll be here with me in California. I love you.*

His words only added to Darla's fantasy—a cute little house with a white picket fence, kids and dogs in the front yard. Although Darla thought about Jesse constantly, she had not yet devised a plan for them to be together.

My home is here—my parents and friends. I still have to finish graduate school. What about my career goals?

8

May 1971

Darla put all her energy into her studies and maintained a 4.0 average. Her teachers not only recognized her high academic achievements, but also her potential for success. Her hooding ceremony was a valuable opportunity for her family, teachers, mentors, and colleagues to recognize the dedication, effort, and intellect she brought to her work here. To try to win their daughter back, her parents bought her a red Impala convertible. At last, Darla stood at her graduation ceremony. When her name was called, she stepped forward to be hooded. She heard clapping. Someone clapped louder and longer than the others in the audience. Straining her eyes to see who it might be, her heart stopped. Jesse. He waited in the background while her parents, teachers, and friends congratulated her. Amy ran over and hugged Darla. "So happy for my very best friend. Come over after you leave here."

Grinning like the Cheshire cat, Jesse approached her. "Hi, beautiful. I am so proud of you. You are not only lovely, but you are super smart."

Hardly able to speak, Darla mumbled, "Thank you for coming."

"I would never miss this opportunity to celebrate you. That's what I'd like to do—celebrate."

"I have a few parties I need to at least show up for. After that, the night is yours."

On the way out of the auditorium, they passed her parents and her brother.

"Hi, Jesse. How are you?" David asked.

"Fine. I had to come and see Darla receive her master's degree."

Her parents looked at each other, obviously confused. Her dad shook his head and shrugged.

"Oh, Mom and Dad, this is my friend, Jesse."

Her parents forced a smile. "Glad to meet you."

"We are going to some parties. I'll be home late."

"Have fun." Her parents stared at one another.

Jesse took Darla by the hand as he walked her to his rental car. Darla could hardly breathe.

He must care. He came all the way from California to see me receive my master's degree. He must love me.

When they got into the car, Jesse gently kissed her on the cheek.

"I'm so proud of my girl."

"Thanks," was all Darla could say. Her mouth was dry and she couldn't form words.

"Where to?"

"Huh?"

"Where do you want to go first?"

"Let's go to my best friend Amy's house. She wanted me to stop over."

When they arrived at Amy's house, she opened the door and hugged Darla. "Congratulations."

Amy tilted her head and looked at Jesse. "Wow. You made it."

"I couldn't miss celebrating Darla. She's quite a girl."

"That she is."

They spent about an hour at Amy's. Amy handed Darla a present. Darla opened the box. It was a gold charm bracelet with a charm that said best friends.

Darla hugged Amy. "I love it. Thanks so much."

After an hour they said good-bye to Amy and then dropped into two parties where they stayed about thirty minutes at each.

Jesse pulled Darla aside. "I'd like to just spend some time alone with you. Is there a place we can go to talk?"

"Sure. There's little jazz club on the water. They have tables outside, but you can still faintly hear the music. It's open late."

They arrived at *Antons* and requested a quiet table outside. The mellow jazz music played softly in the background. Jesse ordered a bottle of white Zinfandel and fried calamari.

After they finished the food, Jesse took her hand. The same tingling Darla felt the first time he touched her shot through her body.

"Darla, I haven't stopped thinking about you since the

day we said good-bye. I don't want to be this far away from you again. I am asking—will you please come to California and live with me."

Jesse caught her off guard. She stared at him with her mouth open.

"With your degree you won't have any trouble getting a good job."

Darla sighed. "I don't know. Leave my family? Leave my home?"

"Darla, didn't you miss me?"

"Yes. I, too, thought about you all the time." *California. A life with Jesse. Sounds wonderful.*

"Listen, I have an idea. Let's go back to my hotel. I brought some information I got from the counselors at UCLA on job openings in my area that you may qualify for. How does that sound?"

"Let's go for it."

Back at the hotel, they looked over the jobs in psychology Jesse found. One in particular in Venice, near Santa Monica, sounded just like what she was looking for. He also brought a Los Angeles county phone book for her to research.

"I'm flying home tomorrow. I'll give you a chance to think about it. If you decide to come to California, I'll fly back and drive you and your things to California."

"You would do that for me?"

"Yes, my love."

Jesse slowly lifted Darla to her feet. He came to her with all his desire. Together they succumbed to their passion deep into the night. Finding each other again.

Light seeping in the window roused Darla. She found herself enveloped in Jesse's arms. She stretched her neck to check the time—4:30 a.m. She knew she must awaken Jesse. It was time for her to go home. *A few more minutes.* She glanced over at his perfectly built body. His face was so peaceful. He resembled a small boy except for the stubble on his chin. *What an incredibly handsome man he is.* Darla breathed in the scent of him as she caressed his angular cheekbones.

"Wake up sleepy head. It's almost dawn." A gleam of delight turned into a crooked smile.

"Good morning, beautiful."

He gently kissed her neck, then her lips. Neither wanted to stop. It was Jesse who pulled away.

"I don't want your parents calling the police."

As they were getting ready to leave, Jesse whispered, "Please come to California. I would love to wake up every morning with you in my arms."

Darla wanted the same thing.

When Jesse pulled up to Darla's house, she covered her mouth and yawned.

"Go get some sleep, my love. I'll call you later before my plane leaves."

He kissed her quickly and she hugged him back.

"I love you, Jesse."

His words mirrored her own. "Love you back."

I'm happiest when I'm around him. Could we make this work?

9

Darla crept into her house. The question she asked herself resonating in her head. With all this on her mind, she was thankful everyone was still asleep. She tiptoed to her room, threw on a nightgown, and crawled into bed. She could still taste Jesse. His smell lingered in her hair.

The ring of the phone next to her bed startled her out of her sleep. She sat up.

"Hello."

"Hi, babe. I'm at the airport. My plane takes off in an hour."

"Jesse, what time is it?"

"6:00."

"At night?"

"Yes."

"Oh my! I slept all day."

"Darla, you probably needed it. Please make those inquires about a job. I want you with me in California."

"I want to be there with you too. I'm going to send out letters applying for the jobs as soon as possible, Jesse."

"That's my girl."

"I never realized the career opportunities for someone with a master's degree in psychology. The job as a psychologist for a business organization pays the most. Jesse, the job at the clinic is right near Santa Monica where you live. That would be the best."

"I hope something works out for you. I'll phone you soon, my love."

Darla hung up. *My love.* She jumped out of bed, took a shower, and went downstairs. Her parents left a note on the counter:

*Dining with some of Dad's associates.
There's some left over lasagna in the refrigerator.*

She was glad she had the house to herself—she could think. Darla decided not to mention anything about moving until she secured a job. She phoned Amy.

"Hey girl, what are you doing?"

"Nothing. I'm off today. Want to come over and hang out? I assume Jesse's left. So cool he came out for you."

"Yeah, that was a real surprise. I'll see you in about thirty minutes."

Darla put on a little makeup, pulled her hair up in a ponytail, and scribbled a quick note to her parents:

Out with Amy. See you soon.

She found Amy sitting on the porch when she arrived at her house.

"My mom's out for the evening. We have the whole house to ourselves. Or we can go downtown and hang out at the malt shop."

"Let's just stay here. I've got something to share with you. I need your opinion. Jesse wants me to move to California, get a job, and move in with him."

"Groovy. He's adorable."

"I know. But that's not everything."

"You're right. What's the worse thing that could happen? You break up. But listen, you'd be in California with a good job. I wish I could move to California. I have to stay here and help my mother out. Actually, I love it here. For you, this is an opportunity of a lifetime. Go for it."

"First, I need to find a job. I don't want Jesse supporting me. I'd like you to help me write my resume. I brought a copy of my transcript. I'd like to use your electric typewriter to write my cover letter. Tomorrow, I'm going to the placement office at Sarah Lawrence and speak to a counselor to see if they can find any more jobs I'm qualified for in southern California."

"Sounds good, after we work on this, why don't you spend the night. We can watch a movie and make some popcorn."

"Okay."

Darla phoned home. No one answered. She left a message:

Hi Mom. Spending the night at Amy's. See you in the morning.

"Amy, I don't know why I bother checking in. They're always out wining and dining Dad's business associates.

They really have no time for me. Why not move to California with someone who wants to be with me."

"I understand. Let's get this resume done. I picked out an awesome movie."

After the movie, Darla fell asleep dreaming of Jesse's strong arms holding her.

10

The next morning, the girls decided to go to breakfast before they headed over to Sarah Lawrence. Darla and Amy wore the same size. She borrowed a pair of shorts and a tank top after they showered.

At the café, both girls ordered bagels with cream cheese and coffee. Darla looked up from sipping her coffee. "Amy, there's something I need to tell you. I went all the way with Jesse. I know I should have waited until marriage. But I'm sure he loves me. At the moment, it just felt right."

"I know."

"You know?"

"Friends know these things. I think he loves you too. Why else would he ask you to move in with him?"

"I feel guilty. I wish I waited. I knew it was wrong. My grandmother taught to wait for marriage. Maybe this was part of my rebellion against my parents. You know, them planning my whole life out for me. This was something I chose for myself. I'm scared. I don't want to get hurt."

"I do know what you mean, though. I've thought about

this too. I've wanted the whole love forever marriage—the white picket fence—dogs and children in the front yard. I know I'll wait until I'm sure I've found a forever love. You're a strong girl, Darla. I think Jesse loves you. He'll probably ask you to marry him when you get out to California."

"I hope you're right. We better go over to Sarah Lawrence now. I wanted to be there when they first opened. I don't have an appointment. But if I get there early, they may be able to help me."

"Let's go girl."

Fortunately, when they arrived at Sarah Lawrence, the counselor was available and ready to help Darla.

"Darla, we are so proud of how well you did here at Sarah Lawrence. I doubt if you'll have any problem securing a job."

"Thank you, Mrs. Hartly. I am relocating to southern California and looking for a job there."

"Let's see what I can find for you."

She gave Darla three possibilities. One was in the San Fernando Valley, another was in downtown Los Angeles, and one of them was the job at the clinic in Venice not far from where Jesse lived.

Amy dropped Darla off at her house after they left the college.

"Why don't you come by tonight, and you can use the electric typewriter to write more letters to the jobs you just got."

"Okay. I'll come right after dinner."

When Darla entered her home, her parents were sitting in the dining room having lunch.

"Hi, dear. How was your morning?"

"Fine, Mom."

Her dad looked at her. "We are very proud of you, Darla. That boy who showed up at the ceremony seemed nice. Is he from your school?"

"No, Dad. I met him through a friend."

"He sure is handsome," Darla's mom chimed in.

Darla blushed. "Yes, he is."

"Will you be home for dinner tonight?"

"Yes, Mom."

Darla went to her room to work on a letter to send to the perspective jobs. She fell asleep for a few hours when the ring of the phone woke her.

"Hi, my love, how are you doing?"

"Missing you, Jesse."

Darla told Jesse about getting more prospects at Sarah Lawrence and how she was constructing letters to send.

"That's my girl. Right on top of things. I know with your grades and recommendations you will probably get to choose which job you want. It won't be long, and you'll be here with me forever."

After the phone call, Darla went downstairs and set the table for dinner. Her mother made one of her favorite dinners—pork chops, mashed potatoes, and apple sauce. She even made a pineapple upside down cake for dessert.

I wonder what they're up to. Mom hasn't cooked a meal in a long time. I think they suspect I'm planning on moving away.

When Darla arrived at Amy's house, her excitement grew when Amy told her she thought of some helpful information to enhance Darla's cover letter. She told Amy she'd hurry over to the post office first thing in the morning and mail the letters certified mail. Once they finished, Darla went home. Within minutes, Jesse called. She told him about completing the letters and how tomorrow she would send them out.

"The waiting is going to be hard. Just know I'm ready to fly out there and drive your car back to California."

"Wow, thanks. You'd really do all that?"

"Of course. Anything for my girl."

Could Jesse have really fallen in love with me? Aren't things different now? People live together before they get married.

11

Three weeks later, Darla received a response from two of the jobs she applied for. One was for a mental health counselor. The other job was for a clinical therapist in Venice, not far from where Jesse lived. The first one offered her a job outright and inquired if she could relocate within a two week period. This position was in Encino in the San Fernando Valley. It would be quite a commute from where Jesse lived. The latter required an additional phone interview and gave her three possible days and times to phone in for the interview. One of the dates was the day after tomorrow.

Darla barely could contain her excitement. She hurried over to Amy's to tell her the news.

"Hey, that's great. I have an idea. Let's brainstorm questions they might ask you and practice your answers."

"That's good. Let's do it."

Amy conducted mock interviews with Darla for over an hour.

"Thanks, Amy. I feel much more confident now."

On the day of the phone interview, Darla took a deep breath, grabbed a glass of water, and made the call. The interviewer answered immediately.

"Good afternoon. I'm Darla Greystone. I'm applying for the position you have available at your clinic."

"So nice to chat with you, Darla. I'm Ms. Latham. Tell me about yourself, why you want the job, and why you are willing to relocate to California."

Darla couldn't be happier. Those questions were exactly what Amy and she practiced.

After Darla answered, the interviewer continued, "Well Ms. Greystone, to be honest, I interviewed several other candidates for this position, both over the phone and in person. You by far are the most confident. Your transcripts and letters of commendation are impeccable. I would like to offer you the position. Granted you have twenty-four hours to make your decision. Undoubtably, you must have received other offers."

Darla held her breath, ready to spurt out "Yes, I accept."

Just then the interviewer went on.

"I will phone you tomorrow at noon, your time, for your decision. Is that time acceptable for you?"

"Yes, that would be fine, Ms. Latham," Darla answered in a business-like voice.

"Thank you, Darla, for your time."

Darla hardly had time to process what just happened when the doorbell rang.

She rushed down the stairs. Amy stood at the door. Darla jumped up and down.

"I got it! I got it! They offered me the job."

"Oh, Darla, I'm so happy for you."

She threw her arms around Darla.

"Let's go celebrate. I'll treat you to a double ice cream sundae."

"Let's go for it."

Darla could barely contain her joy as the girls talked about her living in California.

"I remember, Darla, when we were younger you talked about how cool it would be to live in California. I think the Beach Boys helped to shape your perception of California by creating its image as a place of fun, sunshine, and endless possibilities. With the great weather, you'd be able to be outside much more than here. You'll be biking, hiking, and hanging out at the beach."

"I need to make this move for me. I want to make choices that align with my own desires and beliefs, not being dictated by my parents' expectations. This is a dream come true. I get to actually live in California with all the beaches, mountains, deserts—and be with Jesse. You'll come visit me. Won't you, Amy?"

"Of course."

Darla wasn't home for fifteen minutes when the phone rang.

"How's my girl doing?"

"Amazing, Jesse. I got the job I wanted."

"When does it start?"

"Not totally sure. I think at the beginning of the month.

Ms. Latham is calling me tomorrow at noon to get my final acceptance."

"I'll call you tomorrow evening after you have all the details. We can make the arrangements for me to come out there."

"Sounds good. I still haven't mentioned anything to my parents about California. I guess I need to do that tonight."

"I hope it goes well. Talk to you tomorrow."

Things worked out. Darla's parents were home for dinner that night. When the meal finished, Darla said, "Listen, Mom and Dad, I've been offered a job as a clinical psychologist."

"That's wonderful, dear." Her mother patted her hand.

"Where's the job located?" her dad inquired. His eyebrows raised.

"California."

"California?" her mom shouted and spit out a piece of cake she was eating.

"Does this have anything to do with the young man who came to your hooding ceremony?"

"Yes, Dad. Jesse lives in California." She continued in her defense. "I've always wanted to live out west."

Darla's mother's eyes welled up. "My baby's leaving."

Dr. Ben Greystone looked confidently at his daughter. "Darla, you need to make a life for yourself. Your mother and I hoped it would be closer to home. We raised you right and we respect your decision."

Darla hesitated. A slight smile appeared on the face. "Thanks, Dad."

Her mother looked at her with a hint of sadness on her face. "We love you."

The next day, Ms. Latham called precisely at noon.

"Darla, have you made your decision?"

"I would love to accept your job offer."

"Terrific. We will need you to be here ready to start work on July fifteen. That's nineteen days away. Will that be possible?"

"Yes, ma'am."

"Here is my home number. Please call me when you arrive in town. I would love to take you out to lunch and get to know you a little better before you start your job."

"Thank you."

Darla was motivated by the prospect of a fresh start, new experiences, and a chance to build a career that aligned with her goals.

Everything is working out. I must have made the right choice. Why am I filled with such a mix of emotions? I'm so excited for a chance to just be Darla—not Dr. Greystone's daughter. I have a chance to establish my own identity. Yet, leaving behind all that's familiar makes me feel anxious and uncertain. Although things were never great with my parents, leaving is kind of bittersweet. Being with Jesse will make everything right.

❧ 12 ❧

Darla bounced out of bed that morning when the phone rang. Breathless with excitement, she knew it had to be Jesse. After all, he had promised to call.

She picked up the receiver and shouted into the phone, "Hello, Jesse. I accepted the job. She wants me out there by the fifteenth."

"I can fly out on Friday. Will that give you enough time to get your things ready?"

"Yes, I can do that."

"We can do some site seeing on this trip across country. How does that sound to you, Darla?'

"Jesse, that sounds like fun. My brother gave me a 35mm camera for graduation. I can take lots of pictures."

"You'll probably need to have an oil change done on your car."

"Okay, thanks. Can't wait to see you, Jesse."

"Bye, love."

Darla's dad took care of the maintenance on her car and

filled the gas tank. He also gave her three hundred dollars for gas.

Jesse booked a flight to La Guardia and a room at a Holiday Inn near the airport. Darla wanted to spend that night going out to dinner with her family.

Darla picked Jesse up at sunrise the next day. They planned to get an early start.

They drove right to Darla's house to get her things and pack up the car.

She noticed Amy and David waiting there with her parents.

Darla's mom told Jesse, "Take care of my daughter, phone us every day, and please take your time driving."

Jesse assured them, "We plan on stopping in Nashville, the Grand Canyon, and Zion National Park. Darla said she's never been to those places. I want the trip to be memorable for her."

"Yes. Just remember Darla needs to be there in time for her job," her dad reminded them.

"Yes, sir. I'll see to that."

Amy walked over to Darla. The girls embraced.

"I want you to know, Darla, how much I care for you and value our friendship."

"Me too, Amy, you'll always be my best friend wherever I am. I'll never forget our amazing times together."

Tears streamed down Darla's cheeks. She hugged her parents and David. Her mom hugged Jesse.

Her dad shook his hand and looked straight into his eyes.

"You better not hurt my daughter."

"I don't plan on doing that, Dr. Greystone."

Darla wondered why her parents never asked where she would be living. She knew they already figured it out. She waved good-bye as they climbed into the car.

The drive across the United States turned into an adventure Darla would never forget. She documented the journey with a Minolta 35mm camera her brother gave her for graduation. She brought enough film to take hundreds of photos. Darla's favorite stop was Zion National Park.

"Jesse, I read somewhere that there are black bears in the park. Do you think we'll get to see any? I love black bears."

"Not likely, Darla. Black bears typically avoid humans and will often run away if they sense a human presence."

Darla let out a heavy sigh. "Too bad."

She loved the hike they took on the Emerald Pools Trail. Jesse took pictures of Darla at the sparkling pool. Darla giggled and got into all kinds of funny positions. She clapped her hands together when Jesse bought her some cool souvenirs—picture frames with scenes from the attractions they visited.

"I love this one that says 'Take a hike' featuring the Emerald Pool and pair of hiking boots."

"I know you'll have great pictures to put in them."

On the evening of the seventh day of their trip, they arrived in Santa Monica. Darla gasped and stood with her mouth wide open when they walked into Jesse's place. It was the largest condominium she ever saw with an unobstructed ocean view. There was marble countertops with elegant furnishings.

"I guess you're wondering how I'm affording all this. My parents are filthy rich. They own this unit."

"They must be. I've never seen a college student's apartment furnished like this."

"Here, let me show you around."

Darla's eyes widened when Jesse took her into the master bedroom. It was huge. There against a wall was a California king waterbed with an animal fur bedspread. On another wall was a sliding glass door with a balcony looking out at the ocean. The room had a walk-in closet that could have been another room. In the bathroom were two separate counters with a glass shower and a separate jacuzzi tub. The second bedroom was nothing fancy. Around the corner from the formal dining room was the room Jesse referred to as his man cave—with a pool table, television, pinball machine, and juke box.

Darla went to take a shower. When she came out, she found Jesse asleep on the bed. After removing his shoes, she climbed in beside him and fell asleep.

13

July 1971

*D*arla awoke the next morning to the smell of bacon. She rolled over to see Jesse all showered and dressed standing in the doorway.

"Wake up, sleepyhead. Breakfast is ready."

She got up, put on her robe, and walked out into the kitchen. The table was set. He also placed flowers in a vase in the center.

"I cooked breakfast. I hope you like bacon, cheese, and avocado omelet. Here's some fresh squeezed orange juice."

"Thanks, Jesse. It looks yummy."

When they finished eating, Jesse said, "Hurry up and get ready, I want to show you around."

Darla hurried and took a quick shower and pulled her hair up in a ponytail. She applied a little mascara, threw on a pair of white shorts and a pink tank top. Jesse took her by the hand. She jumped in the front seat of his car.

Their first stop was the Santa Monica pier. Darla fell into Jesse's arms and kissed him.

"I feel like I'm really in California now."

"This is one of the city's earliest landmarks. Next, let's drive down to Venice beach."

"Jesse, this is such a fun cool place."

"Yeah, we can come here to bicycle, skate, play volley-ball, or just hang out on the beach."

For lunch, Jesse took her to the infamous Meatless Mess Hall on the ocean front walk. He ordered her a Too Much Crunch entrée—rice cakes, almonds, tomatoes, cheddar cheese, garlic, and homemade mayonnaise. They split a Kale Mushroom Garbanzo Bean salad with avocado dressing.

"This is amazing. I never ate anything like this."

"California is known for health food restaurants. I eat at them every chance I get."

After they finished eating, Jesse drove northwest down Pacific Coast Highway to Malibu Beach.

Jesse parked the car, walked around, and opened the door. He took her by the hand.

"Let's walk down the beach."

"Okay."

The weather was perfect. Darla loved walking on the warm sand. She stuck her feet into the chilly water.

"The ocean is colder here on the west coast."

Jesse had brought a blanket, and they sat and watched the surfers. Darla looked around. "Those are gorgeous homes up from the beach on the cliffs."

"Those homes belong to celebrities. See that home to the left of us. It belongs to Steve McQueen."

"Wow. What a beautiful place for a home."

Jesse and Darla walked about two miles up and down the beach.

"Hey, I have a surprise for you."

"You do?"

"You're going to get to meet my parents. It's my dad's birthday, and my mom is throwing a catered affair."

"Oh my! Do I need to dress up?"

"I'm going to run back to the house. You could wear a cute summer dress. I'll probably put on some Levis and a Hawaiian print shirt."

"Will Autumn and Jamie be there?"

"Of course."

"I won't be too nervous then."

"Nervous about what?"

'What if your parents don't like me?'

"Sure they'll like you because I like you."

She leaned over and gave Jesse a kiss on his cheek. He squeezed her hand.

When they arrived at Jesse's parents' home in Calabasas, Darla's eyes widened and she let out a gasp. "I can't believe it! You didn't prepare me. Jesse, you told me they were rich, but I didn't expect this."

The home was gated in a canyon-like setting—large oak trees leading up to the house. Around the pool and spa were lush landscaping and a separate garden area. *They must be millionaires.* The house had five bedrooms, five bathrooms, a chef's kitchen, and a very large game room. The floors were marble with high ceilings and magnificent chandeliers. Jesse's mother, Jill, greeted them at the front door.

"This is Darla, Mom."

"Welcome to our home, my dear."

His mother was dressed in a flowing white dress that accentuated her tan. She was tall and thin with frosted shoulder-length hair. She had striking teal eyes. What Darla noticed was the ring on her hand. It had to be three or more carats.

Jill took Darla by the arm.

"Come, dear. You must meet Jesse's father. Fred, this is Darla, the girl Jesse traveled all over the country for."

"Well, she's pretty enough. I don't blame the boy."

Darla blushed as Fred gave her the once over. Jesse's dad reminded her of Clark Gable in *Gone With the Wind*—his dark hair brushed across his forehead. He had dimples, a slight mustache, and piercing dark eyes.

When Jaime and Autumn arrived, Darla relaxed a little to have someone familiar to talk with.

Autumn wore a pale blue angel blouse with a white mini skirt. She hugged Darla.

"So glad you finally made it here."

Jamie gave her a kiss on the check. "Hey girl, good to have you in Cali."

The caterer arrived with mounds of food—everything from shrimp cocktail to steak kabobs. The birthday cake was Tiramisu. Darla loved it. She had never tasted it before. She ate two pieces and even asked Jesse to bring a piece home when his mom loaded both boys with take-home plates.

14

Filled with anticipation, Darla arrived early the next day at the restaurant to meet with her new supervisor, Janet Latham. Darla pulled her hair up in a bun and wore a light blue pantsuit hoping to appear more businesslike. Ms. Latham chose a quaint Italian bistro in Santa Monica for their meeting. The restaurant had rich wooden tables and chairs with red and white checkered tablecloths with soft lighting. On each table were decorative bottles of olive oil. A huge mural of the Amalfi Coast graced the main wall. On the shelf surrounding the restaurant were Chianti bottles with flower arrangements accented with sprigs of oregano and rosemary.

Ms. Latham arrived a few minutes later dressed in a crisp white blouse and a grey pencil skirt with a charcoal blazer. Her perfect posture added to her picture of sophistication. To compliment her stylish attire, her makeup consisted of nude shades with a hint of rose on her cheeks and lips.

She extended her manicured hand to Darla with a confident smile.

"Pleased to meet you, Darla."

"My pleasure, Ms. Latham."

"Please call me Janet. May I order for us both? I come here often."

Janet ordered two glasses of Chianti, two antipasto salads, and the ravioli trio which consisted of spinach, squash, and cheese ravioli. Darla enjoyed the meal. Ms. Latham made her feel comfortable. Darla sensed her passion for her job. Janet told her she must be able to examine the information they collect on their clients and draw conclusions to hopefully help them.

"You must be an active listener, be empathic, and patient. In our line of work, we must be lifelong learners always examining new theories and knowledge to diagnose and treat our client's conditions."

Darla immediately respected and liked Ms. Latham. She felt she could learn so much from her.

After thanking Ms. Latham for lunch, Darla suddenly felt different.

I'm a professional now.

She could see herself in the future like Ms. Latham. Any apprehension she had about starting her career now changed to excitement. She couldn't wait to get home and share the news with Jesse.

When Darla entered the house, Jesse's eyebrow went up. He stood there nodding his head with a beaming smile. "You look slick."

"Slick?"

"Sophisticated—your hair up—wearing a business suit."

"I have to look professional now that I'm going to be working as a psychologist."

He tugged at her hair until it fell loosely around her shoulders. Gently, Jesse ran his hand through her hair. Then he took her gently by the hand.

"Well, doctor, I have a problem now. I think you can help me with it."

He led her into the bedroom.

I've made Jesse proud again.

A week later, Darla started her new job. She not only loved the job, but she liked all her co-workers. Besides Janet Latham, there was Cindy, a bubbly redhead who loved working with children. Also, there was Arthur, an ex-marine, who worked mostly with battle fatigue cases. Jesse made Darla feel adored. Every holiday and weekend he would plan a new adventure for them. He took her all over California. Her favorite excursion was to Yosemite National Park—the giant sequoias and countless waterfalls. The cozy cabin they stayed in truly made it a wilderness experience. The entire cabin inside and out was log with a stone fireplace and a wraparound porch. After an incredible day of hiking, the fireplace enhanced their romance.

Darla lay awake watching Jesse sleep thinking how childlike he looked. Although she still sometimes questioned moving in together, Darla was certain it deepened their intimacy and closeness and created a stronger bond between them.

Everybody's living together now in the '70s. I think he

really loves me and wants to be with me forever. Eventually, he'll ask me to marry him. Why do I worry so much about Jesse's commitment? Why can't I just relax and enjoy the adventure.

∽ 15 ∽

October 1972

After a little over a year of living in California with Jesse, things seemed different. Darla always brought her reports home to work on. Jesse had never complained before. He kept himself busy at the gym or doing his own schoolwork.

Lately, he would grumble, "All you seem to care about is that job. That's all you talk about, and you're always taking work home. You don't want to have fun anymore."

"Jesse, we do fun things on the weekends. I have a job now and responsibilities."

Darla began to realize that all Jesse cared about was a good time. One of the things he found pleasurable was smoking pot every chance he got. Darla often gave in and smoked with him on weekends. Now she had something to lose—it was illegal. If she brought that up to Jesse, it started an argument.

"You sound like my parents. Don't go paranoid on me."
If there wasn't a party to go to, Jesse would throw one.

At the end of October, Jesse's parents went to the south of France for two weeks. Jesse planned a Halloween pool party at their house. He made sure lots of pizza and kegs of beer were delivered. When it started to get dark, he insisted they all go skinny dipping. At first, Darla hesitated. Jesse kept pushing her.

"Hey, babe, you've got a great body. You should be proud of it."

Darla did enjoy how freeing it felt until Jesse was all over her in the water in front of everyone.

What finally enraged Darla was when a much younger girl named Lily flirted with Jesse. He soaked it up. When Lily handed Jesse a joint, Darla had enough. She motioned to Jamie to throw her a towel. She slipped out of the pool without Jesse even noticing.

Darla ran into the bathroom and got dressed.

When she came out, Jamie asked, "Are you all right?"

"No, Jamie. I just want to go home."

"Okay. I'll give you a ride home."

"Thanks. Where's Autumn?"

"She had to work at the hospital tonight. I only came to make sure Jesse didn't wreck my parents' home. He needs to grow up. He's my brother and all, but I don't understand how you put up with him. You're so much better, Darla"

"He's not that bad, Jaime. He just likes to have fun."

"Stop defending him. Like I said, he needs to grow up

and face life. He's twenty-five and still going to college. What's he taking, like six credits a semester? It's my parents' fault. They indulge him. They've always given him whatever he wants."

Darla got home and climbed into bed. She felt angry, sad, and confused. Darla struggled with the feeling that Jesse misled her and that she made a poor choice. She felt an immense regret over the time and effort she invested in the relationship.

I talked myself into a lie. I was committed—Jesse never was. I knew better. Grandma always told me when a man really loves you, he'll demonstrate his love through his actions and commitment. Was all this a wake-up call revealing Jesse's flaws and imperfections. Are our priorities different? I've matured, established a career, and have long-term goals. I desire a more settled, traditional life. He's still a free spirit. What am I going to do?

Several hours later, Jesse fell into bed. She pretended to be asleep. She glanced at the clock—4:30 a.m. He smelled of beer and marijuana.

The next morning, she let him sleep in and went for a walk on the beach. She needed time to think and process the things Jamie said. Even though they were twins, Jamie was so different from Jesse. He finished college, worked as a physical therapist, was engaged to Autumn, and they were buying a house together. Although she knew Jamie was right, she loved Jesse, and he loved her. She had given up her home and family to be with him in California. Surely, he would soon ask her to marry him.

Darla fell asleep on the beach only to be awakened by someone dripping water on her.

"Stop. Stop," she yelled while Jesse shook his hair on her.

"Hi. I thought you might be here. Sorry about last night. I guess I drank too much. You shouldn't have left me. I probably shouldn't have driven either."

"No. You're right. Jesse, you need to be more responsible."

With a childish grin on his face, Jesse pleaded, "I'll try. Now let's go get something to eat."

They stopped at a snack shop near the pier. Darla didn't say much.

"You know I love you, right?" Jesse remarked as he threw his arm around her shoulders.

"Jesse, Jamie and Autumn are engaged. They're even buying a house together. What about us?"

"We don't need a piece of paper to say we're in love. What we have is better. I think marriage ruins a relationship. I choose to be with you. I'm not tied to you by some contract." Jesse made his point.

Darla longed for more—children—a family.

Just give him time.

16

December 1972

By the first week of December, Darla felt herself changing even more. She enjoyed spending time with her co-workers more than time at home with Jesse. Each day, he seemed more immature. Things got even worse when Autumn, Jesse's mom, and Darla started planning on shopping for dresses for Autumn's wedding. Jesse's mom kept questioning him about when he was going to make the move to make it legal with Darla. He assumed Darla put her up to it. He was angry all the time.

When she brought him to a Christmas staff party on December 16, he just sat there and couldn't relate. She asked him to dress up a little. Instead, he wore a tie-dyed shirt and jeans. He thought he looked cool. He embarrassed her and was completely out of place. To make things worse, Jesse made derogatory comments about her co-workers on the way home.

"I don't know how you work with those people. They're snobby, and all they talk about is work."

Darla decided not to comment or defend herself. She begged Jesse to go to church with her on Christmas Day. Her parents weren't religious, but her dad always took the family to church for Christmas. She knew it was the one day to celebrate the birth of Jesus.

Jesse said, "Church is for weak people who need a crutch. There is no God. If there was, where was he when my brother was killed in Vietnam?"

Darla refused to argue with him. He just sat around drinking beer and watching football. She was saddened that she hadn't just gone by herself. On December 26, when she returned to work, Darla felt like she was getting the flu.

Ms. Latham approached her. "Dear, you look dreadful. I'm sending you home. Feel better."

Darla never came home early from work. She wasn't prepared for what she found. Sitting all too close on the couch were Jesse and Lily smoking pot.

"Hey, what are you doing home?"

Darla ran to the bathroom and threw up.

"I think I better go," Lily said as she headed to the door.

"No, you don't have to leave. Darla's cool."

Those were the words she heard as she exited the bathroom. Furious but sick, she went into the guest bedroom and slammed the door.

"Babe, what's wrong? Why are you home so early?"

"I'm sick. Leave me alone. I can't believe you have that girl in our home while I'm at work."

"She's my friend."

Darla spent the day in bed. Autumn came to check up on her. She brought her chicken soup.

"I told Jamie what Jesse did with that girl. He said that's not cool. His brother is a loser, and you're better than that."

Those words resonated in Darla's head—*you're better than that.*

Darla's emotional pain of losing trust in Jesse caused her deep sadness and heartbreak. The betrayal made her question her own worth, the value of the relationship, and her own ability to discern what was real.

I'm such a fool. I compromised my own values searching for love. How can I ever face my family and friends?

She went back to work the next day but still didn't feel like herself. She decided to make an appointment that afternoon to see a doctor. The doctor ran several tests and told her he'd get back to her in a few days. In the meantime, he suggested she begin taking a multi-vitamin.

Two days later, Darla was grateful to be alone when the doctor phoned.

"I hope this is good news for you, Darla. You are pregnant. You're about eight weeks into your pregnancy. I'm prescribing some prenatal vitamins. You can pick them up tomorrow at your pharmacy."

"Thank you, Doctor," was all she managed to say. Then she burst into tears.

Pregnant! What will Jesse say? Maybe this is what it will take for him to marry me. Jesse a father? Oh no. I just couldn't imagine that.

Jesse found her still crying when he walked in. "What's wrong with you?"

"I'm pregnant."

"You're what?"

"You heard me. We're having a baby."

"What? Hold up." Jesse's face grew beet red. "We're not having anything. Did you plan this to get me to marry you? I thought you were on the pill."

"I am. These things happen sometimes anyway."

"Well, you need to get rid of it." His voice got louder. "I didn't sign up for this. I'm still young. Having fun."

Darla began to shake all over. "Yeah, Jesse. It's all about you—it's always only been about you—you don't care about me."

"Of course, I care about you. I'm not ready for this baby thing."

"It's your child."

"No. You need to go take care of this."

"You mean have an abortion?"

"Yes. That's right. It's legal now in California."

"You're serious?"

"Yes. You better get rid of this if you want us."

He walked out and slammed the door. Darla phoned work to tell them she went to the doctor, and he put her on medication because the flu came back. She decided to stay in the guest room. The thought of laying beside Jesse made her sick. She cried herself to sleep.

Later in the day, she got up and found a note Jesse left on the counter:

I need a break — Going to San Francisco with some guys from college for a few days to celebrate New Years Eve. Make sure you schedule an appointment to take care of your problem.

My problem?

Darla was furious. She picked up a picture of them, opened the frame, and tore the picture to shreds. Any love Darla had for Jesse immediately turned to hate. Too angry to cry, she phoned Amy.

"That dirt bag," Amy said. "I never thought he'd turn out like this. I'm so sorry. What are you going to do?"

"I think I need to get away from him. What can I do? I don't have much of a choice. I can't raise a child by myself. I'd have to quit my job."

"You could always come home."

"No. That would humiliate my family. Me, an unwed mother? I would be the shame of our town. It would kill my mother."

"Do you want me to come there to be with you? Is Jesse going with you?"

Darla laughed. "Yeah, right? No. I wouldn't want him to. The only part that makes this easy is I wouldn't want a child that is part of him. I don't want to be connected to him in any way."

"I get it. But you shouldn't go through this alone."

"I know. I thought I might ask Autumn. We've become close since I moved here."

"Please ask her. You need someone with you."

Darla phoned Autumn and invited her to meet up for coffee. She told Autumn everything. Autumn kept shaking her head and blinking.

"That jerk. I knew he was reckless and immature. I never thought of him as heartless. You need to leave him."

"I plan on doing that."

"What are you going to do about the pregnancy?"

"Although I don't want to get an abortion, even more, I don't want any part of Jesse."

"I can't blame you. I'll go with you to help you through it."

"Thanks. I was hoping you would offer to do that."

"Right now, you need to go get some of your things and stay at our house."

"What about Jamie?"

"He'll be cool with it. He's not very happy with his brother right now."

Darla wasn't sure when Jesse would return. She ran in and grabbed some things for a few nights.

She'd be back for the rest later.

❧ 17 ❧

January 1973

Darla took a week off from her job for sick leave. Ms. Latham was gracious to give her the time off. She'd never used any of her vacation time.

Three days after she moved in with Autumn and Jaime, Autumn accompanied her to the clinic.

Fear and apprehension gripped Darla as she entered the building. Her eyes opened wide in shock at how many young girls sat in the waiting room. An expressionless woman with bleached blonde hair greeted her.

"All you need to do is fill out some forms, and I'll take you right back. It'll be over before you know it. You're doing the right thing."

Darla looked at her with disgust.

Who is she to determine what's right?

After completing the forms and confirming she had

someone to drive her home, the still smiling woman took her back.

"You can change in here. Remove all your clothes. Put on this gown. I'll be right back."

Darla sat down. She felt as if the room was spinning out of control. She took a deep breath and did what she was told.

"Let's go, dear. They're ready for you."

Darla wasn't prepared for the scene that awaited her. A sudden jolt of electricity coursed through her veins, leaving her momentarily stunned. Along the wall of this big room, lay seven girls on cots with numbers taped to their cot. Darla watched as a number eight was placed on hers.

The girl next to her spoke. "You look terrified. It's nothing. This is my third time here."

Stunned, Darla couldn't respond.

This is just another form of birth control for this girl. Does she not realize what she's doing?

She watched as one by one each girl was taken back into the room where they performed the abortion. They never came back through the same door. Darla assumed there was another room they were taken to recover. Other girls filed in to replace the ones who were gone. Darla's head started spinning again. She thought she might throw up.

What do they do with the aborted fetus? Don't these babies have a right to live? What am I doing here? I know better.

Just as she was about to jump up and run out, a nurse rolled her onto a gurney and pierced the vein in her hand. She looked up and saw a man with a white mask on his face.

"Relax, young lady, your problems will soon be over."

My problem? This doctor is clueless.

The drug slowly took over. Her body drifted into euphoria.

MY PROBLEM?

Darla's mind screamed.

It's not a problem. It's a baabby. It's murder. I'm a murderer.

Blackness.

Darla left the clinic feeling as cold as the table the abortion had been performed on. She moved slowly, as if carrying a heavy burden. She kept her head down, avoiding eye contact with Autumn. Shame and guilt stalked alongside her. Autumn put her arm around her. She squeezed her shoulder for support.

Tears cascaded down Darla's cheeks. She felt like she was walking through a fog.

"We'll go back to my place. Jamie won't be home until much later this evening. You'll get plenty of rest. I'm glad I'm on the late shift this week so I can be there for you."

"Thanks, Autumn. I just want to go to sleep and never wake up. You've been a real friend. I have one other favor to ask you. Tomorrow, Jesse is in class most of the day. Can you help me get the rest of my things out of his house?"

"Of course. I have some Melatonin to help you sleep, and I'm going to make you some Chamomile tea. Is there anything you'd like to eat."

"Thanks. But I'm not very hungry."

Every time Darla attempted to close her eyes and sleep, she found herself re-living the abortion experience. She was sweating and chilled at the same time. Her heart beat rapidly. Squeezing her eyes shut, she willed the drug to take over.

Will this choice I made today haunt me for the rest of my life?

18

Darla slept until early the next morning. After she showered and dressed, she and Autumn hurried over to Jesse's house.

"Yuck," Autumn said, her eyes squinting with her eyebrow lowered. "Looks like he had quite a party."

Darla clenched her fists. A snarl came from her pursed lips. She stormed into the bedroom and thrust the door open with such force that it created a loud bang as the doorknob penetrated the wall. Her heart beat rapidly. There in bed with Jesse was Lily. Instantly, they both sprang up. Lily put her hands up over her face.

"Hi, Darla. You remember my friend Lily," Jesse said with a smug grin on his face.

Darla folded her arms and glared at him.

Autumn took over. "Jesse, you're a real pig. You don't deserve someone like Darla. Let's get out of here."

Lily grabbed her clothes off the floor, attempting to get dressed. She glanced at Jesse.

"I'm out of here." She ran for the door with her shoes in her hand. Looking back at Darla, she mumbled, "I'm sorry."

Darla grabbed her bags down from the closet.

"These are my drawers. Autumn, can you put my clothes in the suitcase. I'm going to get my stuff out of the bathroom."

Jesse walked into the bathroom in his boxer shorts while Darla was shoving everything in a tote bag.

"So did you take care of the problem?"

Darla jabbed her finger into his chest.

"You're not worth an answer." Her whole body shook. She slapped him across the face with all she had.

"You'll be back. You know you love me."

Darla had the urge to hit him again. Instead, she turned and grabbed her clothes from the closet.

"Let's get out of here. I feel sick."

Autumn glared at Jesse angrily as they headed for the door. "You're a loser."

The girls didn't say much on the way to Autumn's. She helped Darla carry her things into the house.

"Autumn, is it okay for me to use your phone to call my supervisor?"

"Sure."

Darla asked Ms. Latham if she could meet her tomorrow for supper.

"Yes, of course, dear. Are you felling better?"

"Yes, ma'am. I just need to talk with you."

Early the next evening, Darla met Janice Latham.

"What's going on, Darla? You look tense."

Darla took a deep breath. With tears welling up in her eyes, she shared everything.

"You've been through a lot this week. I'm here to support you. What are you going to do?"

"I love my job, but I just can't stay here." Darla started to sob.

"Darla, calm down. I think I can help you. Two days ago, I received a call from my friend and colleague in San Diego. She runs a clinic there. It's much larger than ours. She was wondering if I had any openings. One of her psychologist's husbands is being transferred to Los Angeles. They'll be moving up there. I see now that this is providence. We could switch workers. I hate to lose you, but I totally understand. I went through something similar when my husband divorced me. I'll phone her first thing in the morning. Could you finish out the next few weeks until your replacement arrives?"

"Absolutely, I will."

Autumn and Jaime told Darla she could stay with them as long as she needed.

"You're like family," Jamie said. "My brother is a fool. You're the best thing that ever happened to him."

Ms. Latham came through just as she promised.

"The job is yours. I have even better news for you. The woman who you'll be replacing and her husband own the condominium they're living in. Her husband decided to keep it for an investment. They're wondering if you might be interested in renting it. The rent seems fair. I guess you could drive down there this weekend and check it out."

"Thank you so much." Darla hugged Ms. Latham.

The next weekend on her day off, Autumn drove down to San Diego with Darla to look at the condominium.

"Autumn, the one good thing about living with Jesse is I never had to pay rent or utilities. I've saved quite a bit of money."

"Good for you."

The condominium was more than she could have asked for. Not only was the decor and furnishing something Darla loved, but it was only two blocks from the beach. Better than that, it was within a mile of her job. Darla liked the young couple and signed a lease with three months down for rent.

On the way home, Darla said, "In a few weeks I'll be starting a new chapter in my life. Instead of being afraid, I'm actually excited. I'm just sorry that I won't be there for your wedding."

"That's all right. I totally understand. Jamie and I will see you again. Now we have someone to visit in San Diego."

Jamie forbade Jesse to come to his house and harass Darla. Jesse continued to call Darla at Autumn's and at her work, begging her to come back.

Finally, she answered him. "Jesse, we're done. Do you hear me? Done."

She slammed down the phone. She never heard from him again.

She tried to deny the emotional significance of the abortion by attempting to justify her decision.

I am determined to move forward with my life and not dwell on my mistakes. Having an abortion was the only choice I had. Jesse could never have been a father. How would I have been able to work and take care of a baby. It was the most sensible thing to do.

She put on a facade of happiness to hide her deep sadness and anger.

19

March 1973

*D*arla's new job proved to be exactly what she needed. The counseling center that hired her in delightful La Jolla made coming to work a joy. She liked her other four colleagues. They were close to Darla's age. The office manager, Shirley, often presented new research that enhanced her counseling techniques.

The day Darla walked into her new job, a bubbly auburn-haired beauty with azure blue eyes and a perfect smile greeted her.

"Hi. I'm Rayleen Maguire." Rayleen appeared to be around the same age as Darla. Darla detected a bit of a southern drawl. Later, she learned Rayleen grew up in South Carolina.

Rayleen linked her arm in Darla's. "Here, I'll show you your new office. Shirley, our manager, is doing a home study. She'll be back this afternoon. She asked me to get you acquainted. Over here are Thomas and Clayton. They work mostly with battle fatigue patients. We have lots of military in San Diego."

Thomas gave a curt wave. He had dark hair and dark eyes. Darla thought he looked like a nerd.

Clayton smiled and put out his hand. He had big brown eyes and sandy blond hair. The kindness in Clayton's eyes made Darla feel comfortable.

"Hey, Darla, anything I can do to help. Let me know."

"Thanks, Clayton." Darla looked around her office. It had a big window looking out to the city. She loved it. Rayleen burst through the door.

"Hey, I almost forgot. Got you a little something for your desk." She handed Darla a cute black bear holding a sign that read "Welcome."

"Thanks, Rayleen. How did you know I liked black bears?"

"Good guess. I think we're going to be good friends, Darla."

"I'd like that."

"Do you have plans after work today? Want to go to dinner?"

"Sure, Rayleen. Sounds like fun."

The girls met at a Mexican restaurant a few blocks from work. They chatted about all sorts of things. Darla learned that Rayleen liked bike riding just like she did. Rayleen looked intently at Darla. "I'm glad we will be working together. I could use a friend. My husband died two years ago of colon cancer. We met in high school. Married shortly after and attended the same college. I guess I handled his death well because I knew he would no longer suffer. I'm not a particularly religious person but believe we'll be together again one day." She confided in Darla. "My husband Dennis possessed a strong faith in God. He believed until the end. I tried to have faith. When so many prayers for his healing didn't save him, I gave up. It isn't like I don't believe in God. I just don't have time for church and that stuff."

"I understand, Rayleen. I have lots of questions too. My family only went to church on Christmas and Easter. I've never been religious, but I believe in God. I don't understand why he lets bad things happen." Darla adored her job. Shirley turned out to be a fair boss. She always had time for her counselors and their questions.

Rayleen became Darla's tour guide and took her to all the fun places in San Diego. Both girls loved animals. They purchased yearly passes to the San Diego Zoo Safari Park. They acted like teenagers running around looking at all the animals. Of course, Darla's favorite attraction was the bears.

Almost every Saturday, they met for a run or a bike ride. After exercising, it was off to Harry's Coffee Shop in La Jolla. Another thing they had in common was their love for lattes— their favorite.

"We must go to La Jolla Cove to see the sea lions," pleaded Darla every Sunday.

Darla and Rayleen never tired watching the sea lions frolic on the sand and sunbathe on the rocks. Watching their carefree antics made her long to be carefree again too. "I love to listen to their sounds. I wonder what they are saying. It is so cool to be this close to them."

20

November 1973

As the holidays approached, Darla found herself plagued with nightmares. She was awakened several nights a week by the sound of babies crying. The abortion continued to haunt her. She forced herself to keep busy and stay around friends to not be alone with her thoughts. She called her friend Amy. She was the only one Darla could talk to about what she was dealing with after the abortion.

"Amy, I'm having nightmares about babies. I find myself crying myself to sleep. I can't stop thinking about the heartbeat I stopped."

"Darla, I'm so sorry you're trying to handle this all alone. You're dealing with all kinds of emotions—regret, guilt, anger, and probably a lot more. Maybe you need to talk to a counselor or a priest."

Darla's voice got louder. "I'm a counselor. I should be able to help myself. I can't talk to a stranger about this. I don't want to talk to anyone. I just want to forget all about it."

"Just remember, Darla, I'm here for you. You can call me anytime."

"Thanks, Amy. You're such a good friend."

Her parents phoned to tell her they planned on coming out to visit for Thanksgiving. Darla was eager to see them—even though they never slowed down enough to spend time with her—she still missed them. They wanted to see where Darla lived and where she worked. She's apprehensive and hoped they won't lecture her about Jesse. Darla took them to a favorite restaurant of hers called World Famous for dinner the first night they arrived.

Her mother spoke up first. "Your father and I are so proud of your accomplishments. We are happy you are doing well and love your job. I'm sorry things didn't work out with Jesse. Honestly, honey, I think it was for the best. You have a great job here in a beautiful place. It sounds like you found a great friend in Rayleen. I hope she can join us for Thanksgiving dinner."

"Oh, she'll be there. She can't wait to meet you."

Darla's parents immediately loved Rayleen. Her mother remarked about how much she reminded her of Darla's childhood friend Amy.

"You know you're right, Mom. We have so much in common like Amy and I did."

Darla felt sad when she took her parents to the airport.

I do love them, and I know they love me. All the decisions they made for me they felt were in my best interest. They did provide well for me.

Her father's words to her before he left made her feel independent and grown up. "Darla, you're not our little girl anymore. You have grown into a fine woman, and we couldn't be more proud of you."

After Darla's parents left, Darla felt a sense of sadness and loss. Her heart was still breaking and aching over the decision she made to have an abortion. She wasn't looking forward to this Christmas because of the disaster of last Christmas.

I should be feeling joy. Most people are happy and excited about Christmas. All I'm feeling is regret.

Rayleen's parents moved from South Carolina to San Diego to be closer to their daughter after her husband's death.

Darla felt thankful when Rayleen approached her. "Darla, my parents go all out for Christmas. They want you to be part of our celebration. You are invited to a Christmas Eve party and caroling followed by Christmas day dinner."

Darla smiled. *I didn't want to be alone for Christmas.* "Sounds like fun."

"I'll pick you up at noon. Oh, before I forget, pack, you're spending the night. Pack something dressy too."

Darla had no idea what to expect from Rayleen's parents. Her parents Carol and Patrick Koalis hugged her like she was family. They treated her just like a daughter. Rayleen's dad had been a colonel in the military, and he looked as though he could be in a Patton movie. Her mom taught kindergarten for many years. She looked like June Cleaver. When they went into the kitchen, Rayleen's older sister Mary and her two children already were making gingerbread houses.

"Did you ever make a gingerbread house, Darla?" Carol asked.

"No, I haven't."

"Well, pull up a chair."

"You don't need a kit to make one?"

"Nope."

Mrs. Koalis demonstrated how it was done.

"You use graham crackers for the walls, and the icing acts like glue to hold it all together. Next, you decorate with candy and marshmallows." Seven bowls of old-fashioned hard candy, peppermints, and miniature marshmallows sat on the table. Darla and Rayleen stuffed more candy in their mouths than they put on the houses.

After making the gingerbread houses, they baked all sorts of cookies—sugar, linzer tarts, chocolate chip, and almond crescent rolls. Mrs. Koalis prepared a scrumptious meal—turkey, ham, mashed and sweet potatoes, and string bean casserole. Mr. Koalis made his famous eggnog. Darla was stuffed. She managed to eat a piece of pecan pie.

"Wow, Mrs. Koalis, this is the best pie I've ever eaten."

"It's my grandmother's recipe."

"You girls need to go freshen up. We'll be going caroling in about thirty minutes."

As they went to the bedroom to change and put on some makeup, Darla said, "Rayleen, your parents are amazing. They make me feel like part of your family. I've never had so much fun at Christmas."

"Wait 'til tomorrow, Darla. We start the day off with an early church service. That's why you packed a dress. More festivities later. You'll see."

Darla shook her head. "I don't know about this caroling. I can't sing."

Rayleen laughed. "That's okay. It's for the fun of it."

Fun it was. Other neighbors joined them. Houses they sang at brought out cookies for the carolers. One even invited them in for eggnog and homemade scones.

Everyone got up early to blueberry pancakes with rich syrup Mary brought from Michigan. There was a peaceful presence that filled the church. Darla never felt anything like this in a church before. The choir sang songs of praise that touched Darla's heart. The pastor's message was about the love of God. He said Christmas is a celebration of God's immeasurable love for humanity—the gift of his son. Tears welled up in Darla's eyes. She quickly wiped them away before they flowed down her cheeks.

Could God ever love me after I killed my baby?

After church, they exchanged presents. Rayleen's parents gave Darla a cute burgundy sweater. Rayleen bought her a Smokey Robinson cassette tape. Darla got Carol and Patrick a Croft & Barrel serving dish and Rayleen a basket created with pine cones. Rayleen collected decorative Christmas baskets.

Darla was grateful for the time spent with Rayleen's family. She was happy her friend had their support. Determined to let go of the past, she struggled with guilt and shame. One night, the nightmare became more horrific—the doctor's holding up a dead baby laughing and saying your problem is over. She woke up trembling and had difficulty breathing.

Is God punishing me?

21

The next day, Clayton phoned Rayleen with an exciting invitation.

"Hi! I want to invite you and Darla to a New Year's Eve event. My cousin works for a winery, and he gave me tickets to a dinner and wine tasting. It should be great. Tickets sell for fifty dollars each. My cousin is going with his wife. I didn't want to go alone, so I thought I'd ask you and Darla to go. If you don't already have plans."

Darla could tell from the way Clayton looked at Rayleen, it was obvious that he liked her. Knowing her situation, he was content just being friends.

"Thanks for the invite. I'll ask Darla. I'm sure she'll want to go."

Darla didn't want to sit home alone watching the ball drop. When Rayleen called her with the invitation, she was thrilled to be going somewhere.

I think Clayton and Rayleen would be good together. Maybe the three of us going together will let Rayleen see how great he is.

"Rayleen, this calls for a major shopping trip."

"I agree, Darla."

Darla found a little black dress that fit her slim figure perfectly.

Rayleen chose a cobalt blue dress that brought out the blue in her eyes.

Darla said, "I guess all the hours of exercising paid off. I have no bulges."

Rayleen laughed.

When they arrived at the wine tasting and dinner event, Rayleen remarked, "I don't know what's better—the food or the entertainment, Darla."

"Well, the lead singer of the band does sound a lot like Grace Slick. This steak and lobster are fabulous," said Rayleen.

"I'm probably putting on all the pounds I lost exercising," Darla said patting her hips.

"Don't look now," laughed Rayleen. "There's cheesecake for dessert with strawberries. I know that's your favorite."

"I'll skip that. I heard later at the tasting they serve chocolate along with the wine. You know I love my dark chocolate."

Rayleen grinned. "You're right, there's nothing like wine and dark chocolate."

Clayton spoke up. "I'm going to have the cheesecake and the chocolate."

The girls smiled. Darla looked at Clayton and Rayleen laughing together. She saw how kind and considerate he was toward her. He definitely had feelings for her but seemed content with the way things were for now. Darla recognized that they would make a good couple—with so much in common. Her friend wasn't ready for a relationship. Rayleen still needed time to heal. Clayton realized this too and carefully navigated their friendship.

Someone made an announcement. "Wine tasting will commence in fifteen minutes."

They got up and walked over to the tasting area.

Rayleen gasped. "Hey guys, look at all that chocolate."

Set up next to each bottle and glass sat a plate of chocolates. The tasting included four whites, four reds, and four dessert wines. The wine was excellent. Clayton purchased one bottle of white and two bottles of red. He presented Rayleen with the sweet rose wine she enjoyed.

Darla couldn't decide between the sweet red or the dessert wine. Feeling uncomfortable, she noticed someone staring at her. Slowly walking toward her—an immensely handsome man—the very picture of a high powered executive. Glancing up, she noticed broad shoulders, dark wavy hair that curled up a little at his neck, eyes deep and expressive. The kind you could get lost in. With his chiseled lips and bone structure, he could have posed for Adonis. He reached for her hand. His eyes glued to hers. His firm hand warmed hers.

"Hello," the man said. He looked over at Rayleen and Clayton then fixed his eyes back on Darla.

"My name is Giani Razano. This is my winery. I hope you are enjoying yourselves."

Darla could only stare. Her mouth gaping open.

Clayton spoke, extending his hand. Pleased to meet you, Giani. My cousin, Jerry, is one of your workers. He invited us. I'm Clayton Holmes. These are my friends Rayleen Maguire and Darla Greystone."

Giani smiled and brought his gaze back to Darla. His hungry gaze devoured her, looking at her as if she was a slice of pie to be savored.

"I see you are having difficulty choosing between the sweet red blend or the dessert wine. Wait here a minute. I'll be right back."

Darla nodded. She imagined running her fingers through his raven black hair.

I could get lost in those deep coffee brown eyes.

Giani returned. He held a bag out to her. "Enjoy these two wines you were indecisive about. I also included a box of our finest dark chocolates. It complements the wine." Just then the fireworks began. "Happy New Year, I hope 1974 is your best year ever," Giani said.

Giani smiled exposing one dimple on his left cheek. Their gazes tangled for a moment.

"Thank you." Darla smiled at him.

They just stared at one another. "I included a flyer with our upcoming events as well as my business card with my personal phone number on the back. Darla, I'd be honored to have you and your friends as my guests. Do call me. I have to mingle with the guests, Ciao."

"Wow, did you see that, Darla," Rayleen remarked. "That amazingly handsome hunk of a man couldn't take his eyes off you."

Darla blushed.

"Right," Clayton said. "I think he wants to see you

again—his personal phone number. We guys don't do that unless we're interested."

Darla blushed and bit her lip.

"You really need to take him up on it. We'd love to come to another event at a winery."

"I don't know, Rayleen. I don't want to call some man I just met."

They started walking out when Clayton remembered he left his keys on the table. "Be right back."

The girls waited by the door. Darla noticed Clayton talking to Giani. When Clayton returned, Darla asked, "What was that about?"

"Giani asked for my number. He said he didn't feel comfortable asking for yours. He didn't want to appear forward. Just in case you don't want to phone him, he'll contact me about his next event."

Darla pushed a strand of hair behind her ear. She crossed her arms. "Well, he did seem nice."

"He sure is handsome with the dimpled smile and wavy hair," Rayleen said.

Darla gave Rayleen a hesitating nod.

I know I'm lonely, but do I really want to get into another relationship?

22

July 1974

At work one morning, Clayton approached Darla and Rayleen. "Guess who phoned me last night?"

Before Darla could open her mouth, Rayleen blurted out, "Giani."

"That's right. After all these months, he apologized for not contacting me sooner. He invited us to one of his events at his winery in Santa Barbara. It's the weekend after this. There will be a Doo-wop tribute band playing and a dinner is included again. But even better, he said he has friends who own a house on the beach in Carpinteria. They're in Europe, so he invited us to spend the night there."

"I don't know." Darla frowned. *Why am I so scared about seeing him again? Is it his money or his looks. He could have any woman he wants. Or is it just the way he makes me feel when I'm around him?*

"Come on, Darla, it's going to be fun. We will all be there together."

Darla agreed to go. She thought it would be good for her friend to get out and spend more time socially with Clayton.

Rayleen helped Darla pack. She picked out a cute baby blue sundress for her to wear to the event. Rayleen was going to wear a mint green off the shoulder dress. The beautiful drive up the coast and laughing and joking with her friends helped Darla relax.

"I brought my camera so let's stop and take pictures," Darla said.

In Santa Barbara they took pictures of each other with the ocean as the background. Clayton got on all fours and Rayleen climbed on his back. As she was shooting the picture, Rayleen tumbled over with Clayton hanging on. Darla held her side laughing so hard.

When they arrived in Carpinteria, Clayton said, "Giani recommended a sandwich shop called the Worker Bee Café. He said the food is great. We're to go ahead and get some lunch, and he'll meet us in about an hour."

The restaurant was exactly what you would expect near the beach. Surfing pictures on the walls. Woodie wagon miniature cars sat on the shelves. The waitresses wore short shorts and tank tops. Darla ordered a chicken Caesar salad with an unsweetened ice tea. Rayleen chose a cheeseburger, fries, and a cola. Clayton got his favorite—fish tacos and a lemon-lime drink.

Darla finished her last bite when Clayton announced, "Here's Giani now."

Giani walked over with a big smile on his face. His eyes focused on Darla. He wore jeans, a Hawaiian shirt, and canvas shoes. Darla's face felt warm. She knew she was blushing. Looking away, she was still aware of Giani staring at her.

Clayton asked, "You hungry? This place is great. Thanks for recommending it."

"No thank you. I drove through a taco place on the drive up. If you are finished eating, you can follow me to the beach house."

"Okay."

The house was less than a mile away. It had a wrap-around porch and a deck with stairs to the beach. The interior of the house was designed with a coastal theme. The walls—shades of cream, sandy neutrals, and various blues—evoking calm and serenity. Nautical elements on the shelves—seashells, ropes, anchors, and sailboats. The large window created a light-filled, open, spacious feel. Driftwood and coral covered the mantel. Lots of throw pillows in blue and earthy tones lay on the couches.

The bedrooms displayed seaside elegance with a beautiful mural of an ocean scene, bedspreads with blue/green ocean waves, and table lamps made with shells.

Giani smiled with his arms folded. "You like?"

Rayleen turned to Darla. Darla's eyes were half closed with a look of satisfaction on her face.

"It's perfect. Thank you, Giani," Rayleen said.

Smiling wide with his dimple showing, he winked at Darla.

"Well, I have some things to check on at the winery. I

will see you all at six o'clock." He gently touched Darla's arm in passing. "Have fun."

"Let's go for a walk on the beach," Rayleen said.

"You girls go ahead. I think I'll just relax on the deck and maybe get a few winks. Then I'll take a shower before you two hog the bathroom."

The girls chuckled. "Okay, Clayton."

Darla and Rayleen walked quietly along the sand soaking in the ocean air. Rayleen stopped and turned toward Darla. "You know he's smitten with you."

"What? What's smitten?"

"Giani. He's head over heals over you. He not only told Clayton how sweet he thinks you are, but that he is totally impressed with your job. You see the way he looks at you. He looks at you the way a man looks at a shiny new sports car. It's like you're the only person in the room."

"Stop. You're imaging things."

"We'll see tonight."

Darla put her strawberry blonde hair up in a blue ribbon with tendrils cascading down her sun-streaked cheeks. People always told her her hair had a hint of ginger in it. The ribbon complemented her blue sundress. Rayleen's mint green sundress and the rhinestone hair clips enhanced her auburn hair. Clayton wore a Hawaiian shirt and khaki slacks.

Giani greeted the women with a kiss on the cheek and a handshake for Clayton. Looking dashing in a Caribe Italian stripped linen shirt, white slacks, and Italian leather shoes—he looked like he could be on the cover of a men's fashion magazine.

"Bellissino, ladies." His eyes never left Darla.

A crimson color traveled down Darla's cheeks to her neck. She laughed nervously.

Rayleen took her by the arm. "Let's get some wine."

"Great idea," Clayton said.

"I've reserved a table in the front for you for the show."

"Thanks, Giani," they all echoed together. The dinner was served first—prime rib, baked potato, and steamed vegetables with a Greek salad. Lemon meringue pie for dessert. The bread tasted freshly baked and warm. The band came up and sang songs that they were familiar with. So, they sang along with others in the audience. Giani arrived during intermission with d'oeuvres and wine.

Clayton was on one side of Rayleen and Darla was on the other. He sat down next to Darla. Giani's kind of masculinity made every woman at the venue take a second look. In between one of the love songs, he leaned over very close to Darla's ear to speak to her. He gently brushed her cheek when he moved her tendril away from her ear.

"Darla, I'm so glad you decided to come tonight."

Darla's stomach tightened, and she felt her face and neck grow hot.

What am I doing? I should get up and run. I don't want to fall for this man.

At the close of the evening, Giani looked at them and said, "Tomorrow before you leave to go back to San Diego, I'd like to take you all out for breakfast."

Clayton shook his head. "No, Giani. You've already done enough for us."

"I want to take you to one of my favorite spots. I can write it off as a business expense."

"All right. If you insist. What do you think, ladies?"

"I think it would be fun. We appreciate you so much Giani," Rayleen said.

"And what do you think, Darla?" Giani gazed right into her eyes.

The yearning in his eyes gave her goose bumps, and she stuttered,"Sh…sh…ure, I'd like that."

He smiled and touched her arm.

"It will be my pleasure."

Giani arrived early the next morning. They were packed and ready go. "Why don't you follow me to the restaurant. Then you can leave from there."

Clayton spoke for them, "Sounds good."

"Darla, would you ride with me, so I do not have to drive alone?"

"I don't know."

"Go ahead, Darla. Giani's harmless." Rayleen laughed.

Giani took Darla's elbow and quickly led her to his car. The heat of his touch burned into her skin. She trembled like an oak leaf in a storm. They started down the road.

"Do I scare you, Darla?"

He patted her hand.

"Of course not."

"I'm sure you're aware I'm attracted to you. You're not only stunning, but there is a sweet innocence about you. It intrigues me. I can tell someone hurt you deeply. That's why you are cautious."

Darla didn't know how to respond. When he asked if

he could see her again, all she could do was nod. Then he grabbed her hand and held it until they arrived at the restaurant. Giani kept his hand on the small of her back until they were seated.

Rayleen looked over at Darla with a questioning look. "Want to go fix your lipstick, Darla? I'm going to the restroom."

"Okay."

When they were alone in the restroom, Rayleen turned to Darla. "Okay. So, spit it out. What happened with Giani?"

"He wants to see me again."

"I knew it. You said yes, right?"

"I did. But I'm not sure."

"What's not to be sure of. Just take it slow. He seems like the perfect gentleman."

The restaurant turned out to be everything Giani said it was. It overlooked the ocean. All the food was from local farms. Giani suggested the veggie cheese omelet and mango smoothie. Everyone ordered his suggestion. Giani chatted on and on about his upcoming events.

When it was time to say good-bye, Giani hugged the girls. His body clung to Darla. She inhaled his scent.

Putting his lips close to her ear, he whispered, "I can't wait to see you again." Her skin heated at his closeness and sent a tingle down her spine.

On the way home, Rayleen talked on and on about how amazing Giani was and how much he liked Darla.

When Darla got home, she wondered what she should do about Giani.

I'm so confused. I need time to think. He's the exact opposite of Jesse—successful, responsible, a man with a bright future. I think he could be the marrying kind. He's treated me with respect. Why am I worried?

Darla's head hurt from over thinking. She took two aspirin's and fell asleep. Once again, Giani filled her dreams— once again, he held her tightly in his arms. Suddenly, the dream shifted. She was back in the abortion clinic. The doctor was standing there ready to give her an injection. She heard a baby crying. Darla woke up with a start. The dream felt so real. She was dripping wet.

Darla got up, took a shower, put on her pajamas, and poured herself a glass of wine. Her stomach growled. *I'm hungry.* She made a grilled cheese sandwich and a bowl of tomato soup—comfort food. Monday morning would be here way too soon. Darla turned in early. Getting back to work and helping others took her mind off herself and the dilemma she faced with Giani. They met for coffee a few times. He phoned her at least once a month. Giani explained that this was his busiest season.

"I have to return to Sorrento for several months to help my father out at the vineyard. Darla, I promise we will get together when I return."

Darla felt relieved. She had time to sort out her feelings.

Maybe he just got caught up in the moment. I need to be careful. He could have a girlfriend in Italy.

23

January 1975

*A*fter returning from lunch one Friday, Shirley met Darla with a smile. "Looks like someone has an admirer."

She pointed at Darla's office. Rayleen overheard Shirley and rushed over to the office with Darla. On Darla's desk in a beautiful vase were two dozen yellow roses.

"Well, will you look at that. I wonder who sent those?" Rayleen said sarcastically.

Darla picked up the card and read the message out loud.

> *Yellow roses for you my dear, Darla.*
> *I want you to know meeting you has brightened*
> *my world. Will be back in town in a week.*
> *Looking forward to seeing you. XXX Giani*

Darla's hand flew to her heart. She sighed.

He's not giving up.

"I told you he's crazy about you. Go out with him. Let him treat you like a queen. You deserve it."

Clayton walked in. "What's all the commotion?"

"Look, two dozen roses from Giani."

"He's got it bad for you."

Darla looked at her friends.

They mean well. They just want me to be happy. Do I really want to get into another relationship. I'm smart now. I know to be careful. Rayleen's right. I need to be loved unconditionally.

A week later, Shirley buzzed Darla's phone. "You have a call on line one."

"Thanks."

"Hello."

"Hello, Darla." Giani's smooth voice came over the phone. "I'm sorry to call you at work. I arrived in town this morning. I wanted to catch you before you left for home. I would like to take you out to dinner."

"That sounds nice. I have my car here at work. I'm off at five o'clock."

"I could meet you there and follow you home to drop off your car."

"Okay, see you then."

I may as well go out to dinner with him. See if he's serious about a relationship.

Shirley had scheduled a staff meeting that morning. The employees dressed a little more formal for these meetings. Darla had decided to wear a new stylish white pants suit with a blush silk top and black heels. She decided her outfit was perfect to go out to dinner. Darla had also experimented with a new hairstyle that morning—putting her hair up in a loose bun with several strands of hair hanging down her cheeks. Her look spoke sophistication. Giani arrived right on time. He stepped back and took a long look at Darla.

"You look wonderful—very elegant and professional."

Darla blushed and didn't reply.

When Darla got into his car, he asked, "Have you ever been to the Marine Room here in La Jolla?"

"No, I haven't."

"You're going to love it. The ambiance is amazing as well as the food."

Giani was right. Darla's eyes grew wide once the hostess seated them in the restaurant. Not only was there an incredible view, dining at the edge of the beach with the waves nearly toughing your table.

"This is so special, Giani."

"We are lucky to safely be behind glass. If not, we would certainly get splashed." He smiled his dimpled smile and took Darla's hand.

Darla let Giani order. She liked the way he took control.

"I suggest the lobster bisque as a starter," Giani said.

"That sounds good."

He ordered trout with a side of mushrooms and a Caesar salad. He chose a bottle of Cabernet Sauvignon to complement the food.

Maybe it's the wine. Or the romantic view. I feel something I don't want to feel. It's winding through me languid and warm like a tide pool on a summer evening after the air has cooled.

Giani leaned closer to Darla. "I wanted everything to be special for you. It feels so right spending time with you. I want to spoil you."

Darla didn't know how to respond. All she could do was look at him. Giani stared back with a burning intensity in his eyes.

"I leave on Monday for Napa Valley. I would love to spend the day with you on Sunday. We could go to Coronado Island for brunch and spend the afternoon sitting by the pool soaking up the sun and sipping Pina Coladas or whatever you like to drink. My friend is the hotel manager at the Del Coronado Hotel. I can go there whenever I like."

Darla looked up at him. She melted at his gaze. "I'd like that."

On the drive home, Darla laid her head on his shoulder. He took her hand, helped her out of the car, and walked her to her door.

He gently kissed her on the cheek. "Until Sunday, my sweet lady."

Darla walked inside, took off her makeup, and brewed a cup of tea. Sitting on her bed, she reflected on the evening.

Giani was the perfect gentleman. Any other guy would have invited himself in and expected something. Giani is sensitive and well mannered. I've never met such a gentleman. Maybe he's the one who will want to spend his life with me and love me unconditionally.

That night in her dreams, she again was in Giani's arms—secure and comfortable.

The next morning, she met Rayleen at Harry's Coffee Shop in La Jolla to go on a bike ride.

"Tell me everything about last night."

"The restaurant was breathtaking. The food was delicious."

"Did he kiss you?"

"He is a gentle hearted man—not pushing me—for a relationship or intimacy."

"Do you like him?"

"Yes. I think I do. He's taking me to Coronado Island tomorrow."

"Sounds like fun."

"What about you and Clayton?"

"He is definitely growing on me. He's not only fun but considerate of my feelings. We held hands yesterday."

Darla smiled. "Ready to ride?"

Where Darla got home from the bike ride, she soaked in a hot bath, made some chicken soup, and turned on the TV and watched an episode of *Little House on the Prairie*. The phone rang.

"Hello?"

"Hello, beautiful lady. I just wanted to confirm that I will pick you up at nine o'clock."

"Okay."

"See you then."

Darla awoke early. She wanted plenty of time to get ready for Giani. After showering, she put on sunscreen, mascara, and a slight tint of blush. She pulled her hair up in a ponytail. She decided on a forest green one piece with a white eyelet cover up. Giani arrived at nine o'clock sharp. He put the top down on his Mercedes convertible after asking Darla if she minded.

"It's a beautiful day. No worries. I've got my hair put up."

Giani sang along with the radio on the drive out to Coronado Island.

"You have a very nice voice."

"Thank you. I love to sing—especially Italian love songs. I sang a lot at family events when I lived in Sorrento."

They arrived at the Hotel Del Coronado. The valet parked Giani's car.

"We are going to have the Sunday brunch at the Crown Room. It is the locals favorite and has continuously been voted by the *San Diego Magazine* and the *San Diego Evening Tribune* as the best brunch in southern California."

Massive chandeliers hug from the ceiling. Darla gasped when she saw the food displays. On one table was a wide array of breakfast pastries. On another, an omelet station where you could get your choice of an omelet made right in front of you. There was a seafood bar, a candy station, an international cuisine, and even a bloody Mary and mimosa bar. Giani insisted she try everything. Darla ate until she was stuffed.

"Are you ready to go sit on the pool deck?"

"Sure."

Darla picked up her drink.

"Leave your mimosa. We can get more drinks at the pool bar."

"After all that food, I think I might fall asleep."

"Me too."

At the pool, Darla smiled at Giani.

"Would you please put some sunscreen on my back, Giani?"

"My pleasure."

His strong hands massaged her back. Her skin heated at his touch—it thrilled every inch of her body. They both dozed off for about an hour. Darla awoke and searched for Giani.

"Come on in. The water feels amazing. It is refreshing."

Darla slowly eased into the pool. The water felt cool and soothing. Darla swam a few laps, came up, and splashed Giani. He splashed her back.

"Want to take a walk on the beach?"

"Love to."

He took her hand and chatted on about his family growing up in Italy. He told her how his dad took over a vineyard in the states and how it grew into many wineries.

"What about you, Darla? Where did you grow up?"

"I grew up in upstate New York. I went to a snooty all-girls school. My parents mapped out my whole life for me."

"How did you come to be in California?"

"Another story—I'd rather not get into."

Giani noticed a sad faraway look on Darla's face.

"Oh. Okay. I am sorry. I did not mean to upset you."

He spun around and put his hands on her shoulders. She looked up at him with a pleading look.

This man is incredibly male. Everything about him speaks of strength and purpose.

His arms folded around her.

How good it feels to have his arms holding me. He makes me feel safe and secure.

He tilted her chin up and looked longingly into her eyes.

"May I kiss you?"

All Darla could do was nod. His full sensual mouth met hers. An explosion of sensation traveled down her body. Feeling as though she was falling, Darla pulled back. Frustrated with herself, she looked away.

Why am I letting him kiss me. I need to have more self control.

"Darla, please forgive me. I could not help myself. It seemed like a perfect moment. I am not trying to push you. It is just that you make me feel things I never felt for anyone before."

"It's all right. I don't want to rush into anything."

"I understand."

When Giani dropped Darla off later that evening, he said, "I will return in a few days. I would like to see you again. I hope I did not offend you today."

"Yes. I will see you again." He squeezed her hand, turned, and left.

Darla decided to call Amy and share what was happening with her and Giani. Amy listened quietly then said, "Darla, you're my best friend. I want you to be happy. But, please be careful. You've been through a lot. I don't want you to be disappointed."

"Thanks, Amy. You're always there for me."

Darla spent the week sorting out her feelings for Giani. She knew she was falling for him.

I hardly know him. He seems reluctant to share too much about himself and his life. I am so afraid—afraid to get involved—only to be hurt and disappointed again.

When Giani returned a few days later, he took Darla to a movie and ice cream after.

Sitting in the ice cream parlor sharing a banana split, Darla said, "I moved to California with my boyfriend. He hurt me deeply. Now I'm scared of a serious relationship."

"Thank you, Darla, for trusting me to share that. I don't plan on hurting you. In fact, I'm falling in love with you." His dark eyes were alive with emotion.

"I care a great deal for you too, Giani."

"Then let's take it one day at a time and see what happens."

She smiled back at Giani and nodded her head.

∽ 24 ∽

January 1977

Over the next two years, Giani and Darla spent time together every chance they got. Giani traveled a lot, so Darla had time to herself. Their relationship felt comfortable, and it transitioned into heavy kissing. It never went beyond that. Giani didn't try to force himself on her.

During this time, Rayleen and Clayton officially announced they were now a couple. On Christmas Day, he proposed to her. A month later, Darla stood up as her maid of honor at their wedding. Giani missed the rehearsal dinner. He did make it to town to be Darla's date at the wedding reception.

As they danced to "Unchained Melody," Giani whispered in her ear, "I love you. I want to be with you always."

A few weeks later, Giani took Darla to an intimate Italian restaurant. A violinist came to their table singing love songs in Italian.

"This is so romantic, Giani, I feel as though I'm in Italy."

He smiled. "Someday, I will take you there."

Suddenly, Giani stood up. He got down on one knee. Darla's mouth gaped open. Her hands flew to her chest. Her heart raced. "Darla, I have loved you since the first day I saw you. Would you do me the honor of becoming my wife?"

He held up a ring with a huge diamond.

The words stuck in Darla's throat. Her head swam.

"Yes! Yes!" *This feels like a promise of forever. He's committed to me.*

She threw her arms around his neck.

Darla couldn't wait to tell Rayleen the news. She wasn't due back from her honeymoon in Hawaii for a few days. Darla didn't want to bother them. Instead, she phoned Amy.

"Amy, I have some news for you."

"Giani asked you to marry him?"

"How did you know?"

"All you've told me about him, I knew it was bound to happen. I'm so happy for you."

"You will come and be my maid of honor? Actually, Rayleen will be in the wedding party too."

"Of course. When's the date?"

"He doesn't want a long engagement. We set the date for June 1. That gives me some time to find dresses. Giani said we can have the ceremony and reception at his winery here in San Diego. This way all the entertainment and food his workers will take care of. Can you take some time off and come early?"

"I have some vacation time stored up. I will come out for about two weeks before the wedding."

"Sounds great."

Rayleen squealed with joy when she heard the news.

"We're both going to be married ladies. Maybe our kids can grow up together."

The days flew by with shopping for wedding and bridesmaid dresses, ordering invitations, and wedding party gifts. Giani informed her his parents were not well enough to make the trip. Darla was saddened that Giani's family would not be there for the wedding. Only his business associates would attend the wedding. He assured her next year he would take her to Sorrento, Italy, to meet his family.

"We can make a vacation out of it. I will take you all over the Amalfi Coast," Giani promised.

"How would you like to take a ride in a gondola in Venice? Visit Juliet's balcony in Verona. When we are in Tuscany, you will see one of our most beautiful wineries—taste wines and olive oil, see the leaning Tower of Pisa, and the Fortezza Delle Verrucole—a scenic castle in Garfagnana."

Does he really plan on taking me to Italy some day? Why aren't his parents coming to the wedding? He never mentioned before that they were sickly.

With some doubt in her mind, Darla said, "It all sounds so wonderful. I can't wait."

"I have to go to Italy in a few weeks. It's going to be a little longer trip. I'll be gone about three months."

With this news, Darla realized Giani wouldn't return until a month before their wedding. She grew anxious. The manager of the winery assured her everything was set in place. Nothing to worry about.

25

June 1977

THEIR WEDDING DAY ARRIVED. Darla wore a white satin empire waist gown. Her veil was made of Italian lace Giani brought back from Italy. It was decorated with Lily of the Valley flowers. She carried a bouquet of gardenias and yellow roses. Amy and Rayleen wore light rose-colored A-line satin dresses. Clayton, his best man, and Vincent who worked at the San Diego winery wore light grey tuxedos with rose-colored ties. Since Giani was raised as a Catholic, Vincent arranged for his priest to perform the ceremony.

Darla's parents and brother came from New York. Darla noticed tears in her father's eyes when he gave her away. He looked lovingly at her and mouthed the words, "So proud of you."

Giani and Darla faced one another.

The priest said, "The couple have written their own vows."

Giani stood frozen by her beauty. He couldn't take his eyes off her face. "Darla you are my always and forever. My happily every after. My dream come true. My everything."

"Giani, I promise to love you, to stand by you, and always be there for you. I can't wait to face the many adventures of life together."

Everyone agreed the wedding and reception were magical.

The newlyweds left shortly after dinner for the airport. Darla's parents' wedding gift to the couple was a week's stay at the Hanalei Plantation Resort—a luxury resort and spa on Kauai. When they arrived at the airport in Lihue, Giani rented a jeep. The drive from the airport to Princeville where the resort was located took about an hour. Their room was decorated in a tropical theme. Their living room window had an ocean view.

Giani looked around and said, "We can enjoy gorgeous views of the Na Pali coast and sip drinks at Kauai's only swim up bar."

The first two days of their honeymoon, they hardly left the room—only to eat. Giani took his time with Darla. He proved to be a gentle and considerate lover. Darla could not get enough of Giani.

Jesse was a boy. Giani is all man—tender and knows how to please his woman.

They enjoyed every moment of their honeymoon. Giani taught Darla how to snorkel. "It's a undersea paradise. Look at the colors of the fish."

They went sightseeing at Waimea Canyon—the Grand Canyon of the Pacific. One day they packed a lunch and hiked sixteen miles along the Na Pali Coast. When they got to the end of the trail, they ate their lunch and went for a swim in the ocean. A huge turtle swam up to them.

Darla screamed. She thought it was going to bite her. Instead, the turtle just kept knocking into them. After they tired from swimming, they laid down. They sunbathed awhile, then fell asleep.

Giani woke up first. "You are getting sunburned. We better start back before the sun sets."

They got back to the resort, showered, and dressed for dinner. The resort had a small restaurant that had nightly entertainment and great food. The singer sang Hawaiian tunes while Darla and Giani sipped Pina Coladas.

The next day, they went on a helicopter tour. Darla held on tightly to Giani. The pilot got so close to the mountain cliffs it felt like you could reach out and touch them.

On their last night of their honeymoon, Darla and Giani embarked on a catamaran sunset dinner cruise. Giani led them to the best seats on the boat. They had a panoramic view of the Na Pali coast from the water. The chef cooking dinner was right across from them. They served great food—steak, shrimp, and veggies with unlimited drinks. They saw dolphins playing off the boat's bow and sea turtles swimming alongside the boat. The four-and-a-half-hour tour took them to places unreachable by land to see the rugged coastline, flowing waterfalls, and the striking beauty of Kauai.

26

When they returned to San Diego, Darla moved into Giani's house in Torrey Pines. He gave her an unlimited budget to redecorate according to her taste. Giani continued to travel for his job.

Darla busied herself with her job and decorating. Before they were married, she knew Giani's job required him to be gone away from home a lot. It felt different now they were married. She often felt lonesome. Rayleen and Clayton included her in all their activities. Darla felt weird—now that both of them were married.

Giani never returned home without a gift for Darla. The gift she cherished the most came from Terrerosse Sorrento—the maker of unique artistic ceramics. On his last trip to Italy, Giani purchased handmade serving dishes from their store. He spoiled Darla with flowers, perfume, and jewelry. Although she was grateful for his thoughtfulness, what she really wanted was more of Giani. More time with him at home. His job took him away at least three to four days a week—sometimes for a week or two.

She met Rayleen for coffee one Saturday.

"You seem preoccupied, Darla, is something wrong."

"It's Giani. He's loving and thoughtful, but I'm so lonesome. He's gone so much, it doesn't feel like a marriage. I knew his job took him away a lot. I guess I was so in love that I never considered how it would affect me."

"Have you talked to Giani about your feelings?"

"Not yet, Rayleen. I will when he gets home."

As the holidays drew near, Darla's frustration grew.

I thought a happy marriage with Giani would help me to not focus on my past and the mistakes I made.

She wanted a normal marriage with her husband around. Even more aggravating for Darla was Giani often came home exhausted and slept for a day or two.

When Darla voiced her discontent, Giani responded, "Before we were married, you knew I owned wineries all over. My job required traveling. I have given you everything you could possibly want. What else do you need?"

"My husband!"

Giani only shook his head and walked away.

After Giani left, Darla was alone in the house. The feelings of emptiness overshadowed her. The nightmares subsided when Giani was there. Now the nightmares returned with more vivid imagery related to the procedure. She saw babies in pools of blood. The traumatic event was re-experienced as if it was happening in the present. Darla woke up screaming. She was overcome by an intense feeling of guilt and regret over her decision.

I hate myself for what I've done. I can't even pray. God must hate me too.

❧ 27 ❧

December 1978

After a year and a half of marriage, Darla couldn't fight the negative thoughts anymore. Giani stopped making love to her regularly like she was used to. He'd say he was too tired. He wasn't giving her the attention he had given her in the past. Darla grew more suspicious when she found a dry cleaning tag attached to one of Giani's shirts. It read: Calistoga Dry Cleaners Calistoga, CA. The name on the claim check was Sophia Razano.

Darla decided not to say anything to Giani yet. She held on to the claim check. When she laundered his dirty clothes, she smelled a strange perfume that wasn't hers.

The next time Giani left for a few days, she confided in Rayleen and Clayton at lunch. "I found this dry cleaning tag in Giani's suitcase, and his clothes smell like a woman's perfume."

"Oh my. I would never have suspected Giani of anything like this," Clayton stated.

"What should I do, Clayton?"

Rayleen didn't say anything. She just shook her head.

"Why not hire a private investigator? I'll help you locate one."

"Thanks, Clayton."

Two days later, Darla met with Jerry Malone, the private investigator. He assured her he would put a twenty-four-hour watch on her husband. He said, "Now don't you worry. I will find out what's going on."

Giani came home two days later. Since it was practically Christmas, Darla decided not to question him until Malone checked in with her. Giani surprised her and took her out to dinner at the Marine Room restaurant once again.

"I wanted this night to be special," Giani said as he placed a small velvet box on the table in front of her. "Unfortunately, my love, I am needed in Italy. There's a problem at one of our wineries there. I hate that I won't be with you on Christmas Day. I promise to hurry back as soon as I can."

Darla opened the box carefully. Inside was a stunning diamond tennis bracelet. Giani reached over and placed it on her wrist.

"What's this for?"

"It is an early Christmas gift. To show you how much I love you and how much I've missed you."

The next few days felt like a second honeymoon. Giani took Darla for lazy day long walks on the beach. He once again expressed an insatiable passion for making love. Things seemed perfect. Darla almost forgot about the investigation.

One morning, as she laid in his arms, Giani kissed her long and hard. "I'll be gone for about two weeks. I want you to remember this when you get lonely."

His hands caressed her tenderly until they became one. His touch was like electricity flowing through her as her body responded with all she had.

When Darla woke up, she reached over for Giani. He was gone. She picked up his pillow and held it close, taking in the scent of him. Putting the pillow down, she felt a piece of paper. She picked it up. It read:

My darling, you have all of me. Love, Giani.

Darla sighed and closed her eyes remembering how their bodies became one.

Giani poured all his love into me. Is our marriage anything more than passion? I thought Giani was someone who would love me unconditionally. I'm married, yet I'll be alone at Christmas and New Years. And where's my husband? Couldn't his dad or someone else handle the problem in Italy? Something isn't right. Should I be worried?

After the holidays, Darla grew more suspicious of her relationship with Giani. He phoned her often confessing his love—how he couldn't wait to be back in her arms.

One evening in the first week of January, she laid in bed daydreaming about Giani when the phone rang. She jumped up hoping it was him.

Instead, it was Malone. "Darla, this is Jerry Malone. Can you get up to Calistoga this weekend—tomorrow would even be better."

"Mr. Malone, what's going on?"

"I think there are some things you need to see for yourself. I'm sure you'd want to confront them in person."

"I can get off work early tomorrow and fly up there. Can't you tell me anything?"

"I'd rather wait until you get here. Oh, and Darla, I suggest you take a large sum of money out of your bank. You may need the money to hire an attorney."

Although she did not understand his request, Darla decided not to question him. At work the next day, she told Rayleen and Clayton about Malone's phone call.

"We're going with you," Clayton said. "It's a slow day. I'm sure Shirley will let us leave after lunch."

"Thanks, guys, for your support."

When they arrived at Santa Rosa airport, Clayton rented a small compact car. They met Jerry Malone at a local coffee shop.

"Hi, Darla."

Darla looked up at Detective Malone. He was tall and physically fit—able to handle dangerous situations. He had a calm demeanor that made her feel comfortable.

"Hello, Mr. Malone. These are my friends Rayleen and Clayton. Clayton is the one who found you for me."

"Yes. I remember. It's nice to meet you. I'm glad you're here for Darla. She's going to need you."

Darla looked questionably at Malone.

"I'm sorry to have to share this bad news with you, Darla. Giani is married. His wife and two young children live here in Calistoga. He's here now."

Darla's jaw dropped. Her eyes widened in disbelief. Surprise stole the air from her lungs, leaving her breathless. She felt faint.

Rayleen jumped up and threw her arms around Darla. "I'm so sorry."

Darla trembled in Rayleen's arms. "I think I'm going to be sick."

"No, you're not," yelled Clayton. "You're going to pull yourself together and take care of this bigamist."

"That's right, Clayton," Malone said. "In California, the punishment for bigamy is a ten thousand dollar fine, maximum of one year in jail or three years in a state prison. I have already contacted an attorney for you. His expertise is prosecuting bigamists. He's already to jump on it, if you're prepared to proceed."

Darla stared blankly at Malone. Feeling nauseous, she took a few moments to breathe. "Definitely. He needs to pay for this."

Darla's body tensed, and she took a few deep breaths. "I want to see her," Darla said.

"Who?" Malone asked.

"His wife."

Malone responded, "I don't know if that's such a good idea. I don't think you should confront Giani. You need to save that for court."

"I don't intend to see Giani at all. But I would like to talk to his wife."

"Okay. This is their address. Please be carful." Malone looked at Darla with concern.

"We'll go with you," Clayton said.

28

Clayton parked across the street from Giani's house. It was in an upscale neighborhood. No one said much while they waited. Darla didn't know if she was in shock. She couldn't cry. She just felt numb.

After what felt like an eternity, the front door opened. Giani dressed impeccably in a suit stepped out on the porch. A tall, slim woman with shoulder length black hair walked out with two children —a boy and a girl. The boy looked to be about nine and the girl five. Giani kissed the woman and bent down and hugged the children. Darla couldn't make out the dialogue exchange.

Giani got in his car and drove away.

Darla opened the car door. "I'm going in."

"Do you want me to go with you?" Rayleen asked.

"No thanks. I have to do this by myself."

Darla lifted her head, squared her shoulders, and walked to the front door. She rang the doorbell.

After two rings, the woman opened the door.

"May I help you?" she asked with an Italian accent.

"Sophia, I'm Darla. I think we need to talk."

"Talk about what? Do I know you?"

"We need to talk about your husband—and my husband."

Sophia's eyes narrowed. She looked questionably at Darla. "Come in."

They sat down at the kitchen table. The children played with building blocks in the living room. Darla couldn't help noticing how much the children resembled Giani, especially the boy.

"Would you like some coffee?"

"Yes. Thank you."

"Cream and sugar?"

"No. Just black, please."

Darla relayed the entire story of meeting Giani. She told Sophia of their marriage and about his last time coming home. She even took out her California driver's license to prove that her name was Darla Razano.

Sophia folded her hands and listened intently. Then she began, "Giani and I grew up together in Sorrento. We were childhood sweethearts. Our parents always knew we would marry some day. I got pregnant when I was sixteen. We got married in Italy, and he moved me and our baby a year later to America. I know Giani is a flirt. He loves women." Sophia sighed. "Like most Italian men he has had many affairs. It is just something all Italian women come to accept. He has always taken care of me and his children." A slight smile appeared on Sophia's mouth. "He loves me and his children and would never leave us."

"I hope you are right, Sophia." Darla glanced over at

the children again. "You are very sweet and have beautiful children."

"Yes. Thank you. They are my life—Georgette and Anthony. I can see why he is attracted to you, Darla. You are a very lovely woman. I'm sorry he has done this to you."

"Well, Sophia, I'm sorry too. But Giani will pay for this. Bigamy is a crime in California. He probably will go to jail."

"Do what you have to do. I love Giani and will stand by him. I'm never leaving him. He is a good father and a good provider."

Darla gently touched her arm and turned to leave. "I do hope you and the children will always be taken care of. You deserve it."

When she got back into the car, she relayed what transpired with Sophia to Clayton and Rayleen.

"She defended him with all she had. Giani doesn't deserve love like that."

Rayleen and Clayton just shook their heads. "I think you are better off to be rid of him—his lying and cheating," Clayton said. "I know Sophia will contact Giani as soon as she can. We need to get going with this attorney."

While they waited on their return flight to San Diego, Darla called the lawyer suggested by Malone—Jay Herschoff. Malone said he was the toughest divorce attorney in San Diego county. When he was a child, his mother prosecuted his father for bigamy. He has a personal vendetta against these men. Herschoff agreed to meet with Darla early the next morning at his office. He told her to bring a copy of Giani's assets and her marriage certificate.

Darla approached Clayton. "I have an early appointment with the lawyer. Would you and Rayleen go with me just in case I forget some things to ask him?"

"Sure."

Darla liked Jay Herschoff right away—not only was he assertive and confident, he assured Darla he would win. He kind of looked like Robert Redford but heftier.

"We are going to fully prosecute him and charge him with a felony."

Darla moved to the edge of her chair to listen more intently.

Jay looked over Giani's assets. "We are going to ask for the house in Torrey Pines and have him pay the balance on the mortgage. In California, bigamy is a valid ground for annulment, meaning the court can declare the marriage invalid from the beginning. You will automatically be able to go back to your maiden name. To avoid felony charges and jail time, I'm sure he will agree on a large financial settlement. We will be asking for the settlement to be paid up front in one lump sum of fifty thousand dollars."

"I think you should ask for more, Darla, after what he did to you," Clayton said.

"You may be right," continued Jay, "but once Giani receives these papers and is arrested for bigamy, I think he will offer more if we promise to reduce his charges."

They served Giani the papers the same day he was arrested. Giani made bail in three hours. His lawyer contacted Jay Herschoff to let him know Giani agreed to give Darla the house in Torrey Pines completely paid off and a fifty-thousand-dollar settlement in lieu of jail time. The judge collected the ten thousand dollar fine and sentenced Giani to a year of community service at the judge's favorite charity. Giani agreed to it all.

Giani tried to contact Darla several times. She refused to pick up. He left her a lengthy message:

I know you hate me, Darla. I am sorry. I never meant to deceive you or hurt you. I didn't lie when I said I loved you. I don't love Sophia like that. We were childhood sweethearts. She got pregnant and I married her. I've taken care of her and the children ever since. I love her like a sister. I love you like a wife.

After listening to his message, Darla threw up. *How could I ever give my heart to someone like that. I feel so sorry for Sophia.* After that, she blocked his number, and Jay Herschoff helped her take out a restraining order to require Giani to stay away from her.

That night as she rubbed cold cream on her face, she looked into her makeup mirror.

I'm still pretty. My life isn't over because what these men did to me.

Wiping the cold cream off, she glanced into her own eyes.

But I'm different. I'm not the same innocent young girl who left Larchmont. How many more mistakes will I make? And what did I do to my baby?

Darla put her face in her hands and wept.

Several days later, Darla arrived home to find a letter from Giani at her front door. He basically said the same things he said in his phone message. This is when Clayton took over. He called Giani.

Before Giani could say a word, Clayton shouted, "Leave Darla alone. Haven't you hurt her enough. She's got a restraining order. So, if you don't want to go back to jail—stay away. Rayleen and I are helping Darla pack up your things. We will mail them out this week. This is not a warning. This is a threat."

Darla never heard from Giani again. Although he deeply wounded her, she had enough psychological training to realize she was indeed the innocent victim. Her only fault was trusting him. She knew she needed to move on with her life. Darla signed up for yoga and dance classes to channel her anger. The flashbacks and nightmares continued. She found herself sitting up at night wondering about the child she aborted. Darla resorted to taking an over-the-counter drug to sleep.

29

October 1979

After many agonizing months, Darla knew she needed a vacation. She and Amy planned a cruise to Ensenada, Mexico. They booked a snorkeling trip aboard a catamaran with an open bar and snacks.

"Darla, this is amazing. It's like a magical world on the reef. I've never seen such brightly colored fish."

At Chileno Bay, they jumped into the ocean for a close up view of marine life. The sea turtles, the breathtaking sunsets, and the amazing rock formations made the trip a truly unforgettable experience. Both girls pledged to do something like this next year.

Amy still had three more days of vacation left after the cruise. She stayed at Darla's watching old TV reruns and sipping wine. It was just like the old days when they lived near each other.

Amy opened up to Darla. "The things we go through

only make us stronger. A woman's past need not predict her future. She can dance to new music if she chooses. I never told you this, but three years ago I met someone. I fell in love with him at first sight. We got along well—had a lot in common. He was a professional—a dentist. I thought this is it. I'm really in love. He proposed. I said yes. We started planning the wedding. Then after a month, something changed.

"Whenever we were together, he seemed distracted and indifferent. If I asked him a question about the wedding, he'd get agitated and say, 'You decide, whatever you want.' If I questioned him, he only replied he was tired or a lot was going on at work. One week later, while we were on a dinner date, Vince, that was his name, took my hand and said, 'Amy, I can't do this. I'm sorry. I realize I'm still in love with Susanne. She was my last nurse. We got engaged several years ago. She broke it off to marry her college sweetheart. She's gone through a divorce and contacted me three weeks ago. We agreed to meet. As soon as I saw her, I knew I was still in love with her.'"

Darla gasped and threw her arms around her friend. "Oh my, Amy, what did you do?"

"I threw his engagement ring into his wine glass and took a cab home. That was when I realized the only person's reactions you can be responsible for are your own. Actually, Vince did me a favor. He kept me from making the biggest mistake of my life."

"I'm so sorry."

"Don't be. I'm okay. Actually, I'm dating a nice guy named Steven. He's an architect. There's somebody out there for you too, Darla. Remember, you're beautiful inside and out."

"Thanks, Amy. You're a good friend."

"Forever friend."

Darla missed Amy after she left. She felt lonesome.

"You know what you need, Darla—a dog," Rayleen told her one day at work.

"A dog?"

"Yes, Darla. To keep you company. One of my client's dogs just had puppies. She's giving them away—golden retrievers. Want to go have a look at them?"

"Sure."

Darla fell in love with the puppies right away. She remembered Saffron, Amy's dog, how much she wanted a dog then. "You know, Rayleen, when I was growing up, my best friend Amy had a dog that I just loved. I begged my parents for a dog. My mother said no they are dirty.

"I don't know which one to pick, Rayleen?"

"I'd pick the first one that climbs up on you and licks your face."

Darla got on the floor. All the puppies scrambled around her. One chubby guy made it up on her leg and started licking. "I'll take him."

"He's so adorable, Darla. What are you going to name him?"

"Spanky. I think is appropriate with my connection to the characters in *Our Gang*."

Rayleen couldn't leave without getting a puppy herself—a little girl. The runt of the litter.

"I don't think Clayton will mind. We've talked about getting a dog. I'm going to name her Sunshine. Like the John Denver song."

The girls brought the puppies to meet Clayton. "Oh my, look at how cute and lovable they are."

He giggled and played with them until both puppies conked out.

"Will you watch the dogs for us for a little while, honey? Darla and I have to go buy dog supplies—food, a bed, toys, and whatever else we see."

"Sure. Take your time."

Darla and Spanky became instant best friends. It was just what she needed—someone to take care of—someone to love her unconditionally. Rayleen's dog Sunshine and Spanky would often get together for a play day. Spanky offered Darla comfort at night when she tossed and turned from the nightmares. Spanky sensed Darla's anxiety and would lick away her tears.

⤞ 30 ⤝

December 1979

The holidays were a particularly difficult time for Darla. It brought a lot of painful emotions—loneliness and a sense of betrayal—as the reminders of the past were overwhelming. Spending time with her supportive friends Rayleen and Clayton always helped. She was honest with them about how she was feelings, and they encouraged her to be kind and gentle with herself.

Clayton told her, "You don't need someone else to validate you or make you feel good about yourself. No one else gets to decide whether you are happy at Christmas. Choose yourself. Find something to be grateful for every day."

"Thanks, Clayton. Great advice. I'm grateful for you, Rayleen, and Spanky."

After work, Darla took Spanky to the dog park half a mile from her house. He never got aggressive with the other dogs. He just would run and play. Darla knew exercise can be a beneficial tool for managing both grief and regret by promoting physical and mental well-being. Walking to the dog park provided a healthy distraction from the intense thoughts running through her mind. Spending time outdoors was both calming and restorative for Darla.

After going there for quite sometime, she noticed a man with a larger golden retriever. He'd say hi and smile at her. She always saw him reading a book.

One day, he looked up at her. "That's a handsome pup you got there. What's his name?"

"Spanky."

"And yours?" He smiled and motioned for her to sit down.

"Darla."

He grinned. "Oh, I see somebody likes the *Our Gang* comedy shorts."

Darla giggled. "You and your dog—names please."

"I'm Travis Nelson. This is Archie."

"Like the comic book."

"Exactly, Darla. You like to read?"

"Yes, I do, Travis. Actually, I enjoy reading the classics—like *Withering Heights*."

"Only novel written by Emily Brontë. One of my favorites. I'm a publisher. What do you do, Darla?"

"I'm a psychologist."

"Oh no. Don't try to psychoanalyze me."

Darla laughed. "I won't."

Archie came over to Travis and nudged his leash. "It's time to go. Archie's hungry. See you around, Darla." He patted Spanky on the head. "Yeah, see you."

Darla ran into Travis many times at the dog park. Archie and Spanky played together like best friends. Travis started opening up to Darla about his publishing company and sharing the books he read.

"Here, I brought you a book I think you'll enjoy reading. It's kind of a love story/mystery—with lots of twists and turns."

She began reading it that night and couldn't put it down. He was right that she would love the book. She looked forward to seeing Travis.

The next day, when she saw him walking up to the dog park, she ran up to him. "I adored the book. You were right. Once I started reading, I had to keep going until I finished to see what happened."

"That's great. I brought you another book by the same author. She's one of my favorites. That's why we published her."

"I think she's one of my favorites too now."

Travis stopped reading when he went to the dog park. He seemed to enjoy his conversations with Darla more. She felt comfortable around him. Not only was he a good listener, he didn't offer advice unless she asked him for it. Travis was always ready with a helpful smile and a quiet, reassuring voice.

Travis's stories about growing up on a farm in Iowa with two siblings fascinated Darla.

"We had all sorts of animals: cows, chickens, geese, pigs, horses, even a donkey. My favorite book back then was 'Charlotte's Web.' That's why I loved the pigs. One year a runt arrived in one of the litters. My dad didn't think it would survive. Just like Fern, in the book, I begged him to let me try and save it. He agreed reluctantly. I named the piglet Wilbur. We bottle fed, loved, and cherished him like one of the family. Wilbur survived and Dad never slaughtered him. He lived a happy long life on the farm. He died of old age."

"Wow. What a story. You really had a great childhood."

"Yes, I did. My brother and sister all shared similar experiences with the animals on the farm. My sister loved to watch the animals give birth. Susie would put together this nurse's outfit and get out her little doctor kit and be right there to help. She'd chuckle with delight each time a new little animal baby was born. My brother Doug ran around and around the yard so the geese would chase him. They'd knock him down and nip at his sneakers. He'd laugh until he wet his pants."

"Where are your brother and sister now?"

"Doug still lives in Iowa close to where we grew up. Susie went to college and got a business degree. She moved to the city and is an executive for General Mills, a company in Cedar Rapids."

Darla looked forward daily to chatting with Travis. He made her laugh.

Travis told her one day, "I'd like to write a book one day."

"You would? What would you call it?'

"*All I Need to Know How to Live I Learned From My Dog.* Archie taught me to love and give without expecting anything in return."

Darla smiled.

She usually took Spanky to the dog park after work on weekdays and early mornings on Saturday or Sunday. She'd go later if she planned a run or bike ride with Rayleen. Now that her friend was married, Darla respected her private time with Clayton.

Darla grew concerned when Travis and Archie didn't show up at the dog park for a week. She didn't have a way to get in touch with him—no phone number or address.

What if he's been in an accident? Or Archie or him could be sick. Why didn't we exchange numbers?

Almost a week later, Travis showed up at the park. He wore a sweatshirt with a picture of a golden retriever on it with the words Life is Golden.

"Hi, Darla. Hi, Spanky."

He petted Spanky. Spanky wagged his tail and licked Archie.

"Where have you been? You had me worried."

"You worried about me? Thanks. I'm sorry for making you worry. I had the flu. We should get each other's phone numbers."

"Good idea, Travis. I like your shirt."

"I'm glad, Darla, because I got you one too."

Travis pulled a gift bag out of his backpack. When Darla opened it, a bright smile stretched across her face. It was a teal blue sweatshirt just like the one Travis wore with the golden retriever on it.

"Thank you. I love it."

She jumped up and hugged him. He hugged her back.

"Can you watch Spanky for a minute? I'm going to run into the restroom and put this on."

"Sure."

When Darla returned, Travis said, "It fits you perfect. That's a good color for you too." Darla smiled.

"Hey, when we leave today, we're going to get pizza. It's a dog-friendly restaurant. They even give the dogs some pizza crust. Do you like pizza? Want to join us?" Travis asked.

"Who doesn't like pizza, Travis? I'd love to come." At the pizza restaurant, Darla discovered Travis liked pineapple and pepperoni pizza. It was one of her favorites too. The dogs enjoyed the pizza crust and seemed to be having as much fun as Darla and Travis. The restaurant showed old TV shows—*The Three Stooges, Lassie,* and even the *Our Gang* comedy shorts. Darla and Travis laughed and laughed when Darla and Spanky were on. They exchanged numbers and promised to meet up tomorrow.

∽ 31 ∽

April 1980

Late one night, Amy phoned. "I have exciting news. Steven and I are getting married."

"Why didn't you tell me things were getting serious or when he proposed?"

"Darla, I wanted to wait and tell you when I knew I was really ready for this."

"I understand. Thank you for being considerate. Now I can be happy for you. From what you've told me, he's seems like a great guy. Have you set a date yet?"

"Yes. June first. You know I always dreamed of being a June bride. You'll be my maid of honor. Right?"

"Of course. Did you decide on the colors for the brides-maid dresses yet?"

"I'm thinking of a pastel wedding—dresses in a blush pink, cornflower blue, butter yellow, and a sage green. Our invitations are a French blue. There will be you, my sister, my close friend Katie from college, and my cousin Nancy. You have the first choice of the color for your dress."

"I think I'd like the sage green."

"I thought you would."

Darla decided to tell Amy about Travis.

"It's kind of like our dogs brought us together. I swear if Archie and Spanky weren't both males, we'd be having puppies. They are inseparable best friends."

"Friends are good, Darla. I don't think you need another relationship yet. You guys enjoy each other's company and have fun."

"We do and Travis is easy to confide in."

"Why not bring him to my wedding."

"I don't know about that."

"Explain to him I'm your best friend and don't want you to come to my wedding alone. I think you'll have more fun at the wedding having Travis with you. Tell him you'd like to show him where you grew up. I even bet since Rayleen has a dog now, she wouldn't mind dog sitting both your dogs. She's got that big backyard."

"Yeah, you're right. I'll ask him. We're going to a concert in the park this weekend. It would be a good time to mention it to him."

The next day, Darla went shopping for a wedding gift for Amy. On her way to Macy's, she stopped at House of Fabrics just to look around. She spotted something in the material section that would make a perfect gift for Archie. They had material with dog prints and bones in assorted colors. *I can buy this material and make matching scarves for Archie and Spanky.* Darla chose the blue material and picked out some pink to make one for Sunshine too.

After purchasing serving dishes for a wedding gift and satin peignoir set for the shower gift, she returned home to sew the scarves. It only took her an hour to finish sewing them. She wrapped them in some colorful wrapping paper. Darla looked at the clock and realized it was almost time to get ready for the concert. Hurrying she ate a yogurt, showered, and got dressed. Just as she put the scarf on Spanky, the doorbell rang.

"Hi, Darla. Ready to go?"

Spanky ran up to Travis and wagged his tail.

"Hey, cool scarf, Spanky." Spanky licked Travis' hand.

"Hi, Travis. Here."

Darla handed the gift to Travis. "What's this?"

"Open it."

"Wow. Is this for Archie?"

"Yes."

"You made this."

"I did."

"Way cool."

Archie wagged his tail when Darla got in the car. Spanky jumped in the back seat with his friend.

Travis put the scarf on Archie.

"Look, buddy. A gift from Darla and Spanky."

Archie barked.

"I think he likes it."

Darla chuckled.

When they got to the park, Travis set up two camping chairs and placed a blanket on the ground between them.

Archie and Spanky lay down on the blanket. Travis handed Darla sparking water and a bag of pistachio nuts—her favorites.

"Hey, thanks."

The band played songs from the Eagles. Darla sang along. Archie started to howl. The crowd roared. Travis finally calmed him down with some dog treats.

When it ended, Travis said, "Let's go get some ice cream."

"Sure."

Darla knew this would be a good time to bring up Amy's wedding. She ordered a hot fudge sundae with chocolate chip mint ice cream. Travis ordered a strawberry sundae with vanilla ice cream.

Darla started, "Amy called me tonight with some wonderful news. She and Steven are getting married on June first. She's asked me to be her maid of honor."

"That's great."

"How would you like to go with me? As friends, of course. I could show you around the town I grew up in."

"Well, how long would we stay there?"

"Probably around three or four days. Actually, we could stay at my parents."

"Yes. I will go with you. But I'd rather stay in a hotel. I'm much more comfortable with that. I would still need to make arrangements for Archie."

"I understand. As for Archie, Rayleen has offered to dog sit Spanky. I'm sure Archie would also be welcomed at her and Clayton's home."

"Okay. Let me know for sure about that as soon as you can."

The next day, Darla talked to Rayleen. She agreed to care for both dogs. Travis booked the flights for them to leave on May twenty-ninth and to return on June second. Darla gave him her portion of the airfare.

∾ 32 ∾

May 1980

A my and Steven picked Darla and Travis up at the airport. The couples went out for dinner.

Steven and Travis immediately hit it off. They talked about everything from football to fishing.

The girls excused themselves to use the restroom.

"Darla, Travis is so nice. He's cute too."

"Yes. He's a good friend. Steven sure is crazy about you. He's quite handsome."

"I think so."

When they returned to the table, they found Steven laughing heartily.

"Hey, honey, what's so funny?"

"Travis has been enlightening me about growing up on a farm in Iowa."

"His stories crack me up too, Steven," Darla said.

After they finished eating, they dropped Travis off at his hotel.

Darla turned to him as he was getting out of the car. "I'll pick you up around 9:00 a.m. and take you to my favorite breakfast spot."

"Thanks, Darla. See you in the morning." He gave Darla a slight hug.

"I really like your friend. He's very easy to talk to."

"Yeah, he's a great guy, Steven."

They dropped Darla off at her home. Steven and Amy gave her a big hug.

"Don't forget 6:00 p.m. is the rehearsal dinner," Amy said.

"I won't forget. Travis and I will see you then."

The next day Darla borrowed her dad's car. She picked Travis up right on schedule.

"Good morning, Darla. I'm really hungry. I'm in the mood for blueberry pancakes."

"That's perfect. Where I'm taking you is known for their blueberry pancakes. They even put hot blueberry compote on them."

"Sounds good."

When the meal came, Travis remarked, "Yummy. You weren't lying when you said they were the best."

"I'm glad you enjoyed them."

Darla spent the rest of the day taking Travis around Larchmont. She took him by her elementary and high school. "Here's the hospital where I was born. It's where my dad works now as a neurosurgeon."

Travis loved the little shops in the quaint village, and the many historic homes along the beautiful coastline on the Long Island Sound.

They went back to her house around lunch time, and her mom insisted they stay for lunch. Darla forewarned her mother the night before that Travis and she were just friends. She knew her mother could be pushy, and she wanted to make sure she didn't say anything that would embarrass Travis. Her mother proved to be surprisingly gracious. She prepared open-faced turkey sandwiches and a Cobb salad for them. Darla's brother walked in just as they were finishing up lunch.

"Hi, sis. Good to see you again."

"Hi. Good to see you too." She hugged her brother. "This is my friend Travis."

"Hi, Travis. I'm David, Darla's older brother."

They shook hands.

"Hey, Mom. I came by to borrow a tie from Dad for Amy's wedding."

"Sure. You know where they are."

Around four o'clock, Darla drove Travis back to his hotel to get ready for the dinner. Then she returned to her parents' house to get ready herself. Dara chose a sea-foam green dress and beige heels to wear for the rehearsal dinner.

She picked Travis up at five thirty.

"Wow. You look sharp," Darla said.

Travis wore a dark gray sports coat, a light green stripped shirt, and a medium green tie.

"Thanks, Darla. You look very pretty."

Everything about the rehearsal dinner proved to be elegant. There were chefs carving different meats. On another table stood a white and a dark chocolate fountain fondue with all sorts of cakes and fruits. Steven's father ordered Moet and Chandon Champagne—only the best for his son.

When Darla dropped Travis off, he said, "That was so much fun. I'm glad I came."

"Me too. Remember my brother will be picking you up at 2:00 p.m. Amy arranged for a hairstylist and makeup artist to get us ready for the wedding. I'm sorry you have to eat breakfast in the hotel."

"No problem. I probably won't eat much. I'm stuffed from tonight."

I'm so glad Travis decided to come with me. He's making this time fun for me instead of feeling sad and thinking about all the mistakes I've made.

33

At 10:00 the next morning, Darla hurried to the basement of the church to get beautiful for the wedding. The girls were instructed to wash their hair the night before and wear no makeup.

Amy laughed when Darla arrived.

"Ready to get gorgeous, Darla?"

"Bring it on."

"Amy, you're pretty giddy."

"I'm just really nervous. I want everything to be perfect for Steven."

"No need to worry," the makeup artist said. "You're going to be gorgeous."

Darla watched as she transformed Amy into a beauty.

"Well, dear friend, wait until Steven sees you. You are breathtakingly beautiful."

Amy's hair stylist was busy adding a matching hairpiece to Amy's hair. She put it up leaving small tendrils hanging down her cheeks. She was right. When Amy finally got dressed, her veil fell elegantly around her hair and face.

Darla got dressed next.

"This dress is amazing, Amy."

"That color is perfect for you."

The bridesmaids marched out and stood in the hallway next to their partner. The wedding march began to play. As she walked down the aisle, Darla glanced over at Travis. He smiled and winked. Darla returned his smile. Listening to Amy and Steven exchange their wedding vows, Darla felt her eyes well up. For a moment, she thought of her own wedding with Giani—she pushed those thoughts away and focused on Amy. She instead filled her thoughts with only happiness for Amy.

At the reception, Darla and Travis sat at a table with Amy's college friend Katie and her husband Patrick. Not only a fun couple, but they loved to dance. Patrick even pushed Travis out onto the dance floor.

"You're a really good dancer, Travis."

"You can thank my sister Susie for that, Darla. She constantly employed me as her practice dance partner. Speaking of Susie, she'll be visiting me at the end of the month. I'd like to have you meet her."

"I'd love that."

"Great. I'll make a special dinner."

While they ate the wedding dinner, Darla noticed Travis left several times to use the restroom.

After his last visit to the men's room, Darla looked closely at him. She noticed how extremely pale he looked. He also perspired profusely. This made no sense to Darla because the air conditioning was very cold. Gently, Darla placed her hand on his.

"Are you feeling all right?"

"I'm fine. I think maybe something I ate didn't agree with me."

When Amy and Steven prepared to leave on their honeymoon, Darla decided as soon as they left, she'd take Travis back to his hotel room. She was feeling tired herself.

"Travis, when Amy and Steven exit, let's go too. It's been a long day."

"Sounds good to me. Our plane's leaving at noon will come all too soon.

"Look, Travis, Amy and Steven are getting ready to leave. Let's go. I'll drop you off at your hotel."

"Thanks for inviting me. I thoroughly enjoyed myself."

"Thank you. I'm glad you had fun. My brother is taking us to the airport. Be ready at nine thirty. We can grab a coffee and muffin at the airport."

Travis gave Darla a slight hug when he got out of the car at his hotel. "Good night."

"Good night. See you in the morning."

On the plane ride home, Travis hardly spoke. Again, Darla noticed he made many trips to the restroom. Knowing he's a private person, she never questioned him about it.

Clayton surprised them. When he picked them up at the airport—both Archie and Spanky sat in the back seat of the car. Travis got in the back seat, and both dogs barraged him with kisses.

"Where's Rayleen?"

"She has a cold. She just took some cold medicine and is

sleeping it off. She said she'd call you tomorrow to hear all about the wedding."

Clayton dropped Travis and Archie off first.

"Thanks, Clayton. See you soon, Darla."

On the way to Darla's house, she confided in Clayton about her concern for Travis' health.

"I wouldn't worry too much about his actions. He's a guy. We don't talk about not feeling well. I think he'll be fine."

"I guess you're right, Clayton. Thanks for the ride. And thanks for taking care of Spanky."

The next morning, Darla slept in. She was glad she still had another day off. Exhausted from the excitement of the past four days, she just wanted to hang out at home and rest. Spanky seemed content to lay around too. The last four days with the other two dogs wore him out.

About 5:00 p.m. Darla took Spanky for a short walk. Darla's throat hurt a little, so she made herself some chicken noodle soup when she returned from the walk. She went to bed early and didn't set an alarm clock. At 9:00 a.m. Spanky nudged her.

"It's time to eat. Right Spanky?" She fed her dog and took him for a short walk. Darla's throat still hurt, and she started sneezing. She gargled with salt. Then heated up the left-over chicken noodle soup. She climbed back into bed.

The ring on her phone awakened Darla at 4:00 p.m.

"Hello."

"Hi, Darla. Did I wake you?"

"Yes, Travis. It's okay. I need to get up anyway and set an alarm for work tomorrow."

"You sound terrible. Are you sick?"

"I've got a sore throat and the start of a cold. I think. How are you doing?"

"I'm sorry you're not feeling well. I'm just still a little jet lagged from the trip. I just wanted to check in with you and thank you again for inviting me. Is Spanky worn out? Archie sure is."

"Yes, Spanky is tired too. I don't think these dogs slept for four days."

Travis laughed. "Well, get some sleep and feel better."

"Good night."

The alarm rang way before Darla was ready to get up and go to work. Somehow, she dragged herself into the office. After she coughed and sneezed for hours, Shirley recommended she see a doctor. "I'm going to phone my doctor and see if he has any time to squeeze you in."

"Okay, Shirley. I feel miserable."

Shirley came back into the room. "He said come in right now. He just had a cancellation. Here's the address."

Darla drove to the doctor's office. She checked in. There was only one person waiting. Someone holding a baby carrier walked in. Darla froze. The baby started crying. Darla felt like she couldn't breathe.

She ran up to the front desk. "I feel nauseous. Where's the bathroom?"

"Down the hall, Ms. Greystone. I'll knock on the door when the doctor is ready for you."

"Thanks." Darla ran to the bathroom.

Sweating and holding her stomach she leaned against the bathroom stall. *This is crazy. I can't even be around a baby anymore. I can't keep denying how the abortion is affecting me. I need to find some healing.*

The nurse knocked on the bathroom door to let her know the doctor was ready to see her. "Ms. Greystone, are you all right? You're trembling."

"I'm just feeling very sick, Doctor."

He gave her a shot and prescribed antibiotics.

Darla stayed home the rest of the week. Travis showed up in the middle of the week with his homemade chicken soup and freshly squeezed orange juice. Darla greeted him at the front door.

"Thanks, Travis. I'm not letting you in because I don't want you to get sick too."

"I don't want to come in. I'll take Spanky for a walk with Archie and me."

"I appreciate that."

"I'll stop by tomorrow to walk Spanky again."

When Spanky returned from his walk, Darla could tell he enjoyed seeing Travis and Archie. Rayleen called to check on Darla. She told her about Travis stopping by with soup and taking Spanky for a walk.

"He's a good friend to you. Clayton and I would like to come get Spanky to let you get some rest. I think Sunshine really misses him. She keeps looking all over the house for him. I know Spanky had fun at our home. All three dogs hardly slept."

"I could tell. He slept the whole day when he came home."

Travis kept his word and stopped by to check on Darla.

Darla laid low for the next weekend, boosting her immune system. She missed going to the dog park. She knew she needed to get better to return to work.

The next Monday, Darla went back to work. Everyone was happy to see her. She was glad to be back. It rained Monday afternoon and all day Tuesday. Darla didn't return to the dog park until Wednesday. Archie saw Spanky first as Darla walked up to the park. He ran up to her, jumped up, and licked her face.

"I missed you too, Archie."

Travis laughed and patted Spanky's head. The dogs ran off and played.

"Good to see you, Darla. You look much better."

"I guess I looked terrible."

"Not terrible, Darla. Just sick. My sister Susie is coming a little earlier. She wants to stay for an extra week. She's due to arrive a week from Saturday. You still want to come over for dinner?"

"Of course. I'm looking forward to meeting her."

Darla had gotten behind in her reports by taking time off for the wedding and then getting sick.

She brought the paperwork home. She missed several days at the dog park.

Travis called her on Friday night. "Hi, Darla. I haven't seen you in a while. Are you all right?"

"Yes. I'm fine. I just got behind in my reports with the wedding and getting sick."

"I get it. My sister flies in tomorrow. Want to come for Sunday dinner?"

"Sure."

"Okay. See you at 2:00. Oh, and bring Spanky."

34

Susie surprised Darla when they met. She expected her to look like a farm girl or resemble Travis. She was neither. Her own hair was cut in a stylish cut with red highlights. Her brown eyes were almost an amber color. She was tall and slim. She reminded Darla of a yoga instructor.

Hip tortoise shell glasses framed her face. She had on black slacks, a white blouse, and a black blazer. Outgoing and friendly, Darla liked her immediately.

Travis grilled steaks and corn on the cob on the barbecue. He also made twice baked potatoes.

Susie made a strawberry shortcake for dessert. Darla smiled as Susie and Travis reminisced about their childhood. Travis gave the girls time to get acquainted. He refused any offers for help when he cleaned up the dishes. Susie turned toward Darla with a serious look on her face.

"You really like my brother? Don't you?"

Darla didn't answer right away. She wanted to think about her answer.

"He's a good friend to me."

"I think you feel more than a friend for him."

Darla looked down and didn't respond. Silence permeated the air.

Finally, Susie spoke, "He hasn't told you? Has he?"

"Told me what?"

"I'm not getting in the middle of this. I'll let Travis tell you."

Travis walked back into the living room. The unpleasant question forgotten. Darla stayed for another hour just enjoying them both.

That night, Darla couldn't fall asleep. She kept thinking about what Susie said. *What hasn't Travis told me?*

She was determined not to question Travis.

If he wanted to tell me something, he would.

For the next several weeks, every time she was with Travis that question danced in her head. She decided to invite Travis for dinner. She thought a more intimate setting at her home might allow Travis an opportunity to open up to her. Instead, the relaxed atmosphere allowed Darla to open up and share her heart with Travis. Glancing at the dogs, she nudged Travis.

"Look at them—that's what love must look like—contentment."

Archie and Spanky lay side by side—their bodies touching—total contentment.

"I feel like that with you, Travis."

Travis' eyebrow raised. He didn't know how to process Darla's remark. He just didn't respond.

Darla moved closer to Travis on the couch. She put her hand in his.

"I like you a lot, Travis. I think we're good for one another."

Travis shook his head. Concern written all over his face.

"Listen, Darla. We need to talk. I should have shared something with you sooner."

Darla moved in closer to not miss a word Travis had to say.

"You are wonderful, Darla. But we could never have a relationship. I'm gay."

"What?"

Shock broke out on Darla's face. She squinted trying to figure out if she heard what she thought she did. "No. That's not true," Darla shouted shaking her head over and over.

"It is."

It suddenly got so quiet Darla heard her own breathing. She and Travis just stared at each other.

Travis broke the silence, blurting out another devastating statement.

"And Darla, I'm dying."

"You're what?"

"Dying."

"This is too much Travis. How do you know that?"

"I was diagnosed with Leukemia three years ago. I opted out of chemotherapy treatments and used natural products to control it. It worked for a while. Two months ago, it came back with a vengeance. I don't have much time left."

"Oh no."

Darla grabbed her heart. A tear escaped and cascaded down Darla's cheek.

"There's got to be something they can do."

"No, Darla. That's why Susie came to visit. We've always been very close."

Darla grabbed Travis—hugged him while she cried on his shoulder.

"Please don't cry. I'm thankful for your friendship and for our time together. I do love you in a special way."

"I love you too, Travis. You've been one of my best friends."

Travis took hold of Darla's shoulders and pushed her to a sitting position. Looking deep into her eyes, he said, "Please don't grieve. Let's make the most of the time we have left. This is my time. My brother Doug, who's a Christian, shared with me from the Bible that for each person there's an appointed time for all to die. He sent me a Bible, and I've been reading it. He said when he comes here, he's going to pray with me so I can be assured I'll go to heaven when I die."

"What am I going to do without you?"

"You're going to go on. You're going to live—get married again—someday have children—have a happy life. That's what I want for you, Darla."

35

November 1980

For the past few months, Travis' health had been deteriorating, and he grew weaker. A week before Thanksgiving, his brother Doug arrived to help his sister Susie take care of Travis. They planned to stay as long as they were needed. He refused to go to the hospital. Instead, his siblings had a hospital bed delivered to his home. The day after Thanksgiving, hospice came in. Darla visited Travis every day after work. She took Archie home to care for him when Travis started to decline. She brought him back to see Travis every time she visited.

One day, early in December, when Darla entered Travis' room, she heard clapping and shouts of hallelujah. She wondered what in the world was going on. Both of Travis' siblings wore a smile.

A huge grin spread across Travis' face.

"Hi, Darla. I guess you're wondering what's happening.

My brother brought in a pastor, Pastor Brian. He shared that God loved me and would forgive me from my sins if I asked Jesus into my heart. He told me if I did that, I can go to heaven, my eternal home, when I die. Darla, I did it. All my shame and guilt is gone. I feel as though I've let go of a heavy burden."

Everyone slowly left the room as Travis shared with Darla.

"I want you to go to heaven too, Darla. Please ask Jesus into your heart," Travis pleaded.

Darla wasn't ready for all this. She stood glued to the floor not knowing how to respond.

She didn't want to let Travis down. So, she said, "I'll think about it."

That night, Darla felt compelled to stay as late as she could by Travis' bedside. She held his hand. He fell in and out of consciousness. The entire time Archie kept his head on the bed. Travis' hand rested on Archie's head. Darla got up to use the bathroom. When she came out of the door, Susie motioned her into the kitchen.

"Darla, there's something I need to tell you. Will you sit for a moment?"

Darla was curious, so she said, "All right."

"You need to know the truth. I asked Travis' permission to share this with you. He agreed you had a right to know. Travis loved you, Darla. He's never seemed happier than when he was with you. Instead, he believed the lie that deceived him his entire life. One of my father's workers on the farm, Hank, raped Travis repeatedly from the age of fourteen to sixteen. He threatened Travis that he would rape me if he didn't comply or if he told anyone. Right before Travis turned seventeen, I caught Hank in the act. He didn't know I saw what he was doing. I ran to my dad.

"My dad went crazy and went after Hank with a horse whip. After he whipped him within an inch of his life, he chased him off our property with his rifle. I believe he would have killed him if my mother hadn't intervened. Hank came back with the sheriff to get his stuff. He arrested my father for assault. The trial devastated our family and broke Travis. Travis left home as soon as he turned eighteen. He couldn't handle the looks of pity from the people in our town. In college, he delved into his studies. He probably needed psychological counseling or therapy for what he'd been through. Because of what happened to him, he convinced himself that he was gay. After what Hank did to him, Travis never took part in any relationships—male or female.

"Fear of what he was stifled him. For the first time in his life, Travis experienced freedom today. Freedom came from what the pastor shared with him. He wasn't gay and wasn't responsible for what happened to him. He's free from accountability and humiliation."

Tears welled in Darla's eyes. Poor Travis.

What kind of an animal was Hank to ruin a little boy and hurt him as a man so that he could never have a normal relationship?

Darla hugged Susie. "Thank you so much for sharing this with me."

Doug ran into the kitchen. "Travis is calling for you, Darla."

Darla rushed into Travis' room. She sat on his bed—took him by the hand.

"I'm here, Travis."

"Darla, I love you—please come to heaven. Take care of Archie. He loves you too."

Darla choked back the tears.

"I will, Travis."

Darla slowly exited the room as Travis' siblings came in. She sat on a kitchen chair. Only a few minutes later, Archie began to howl. Darla looked up as Susie walked into the room and nodded her head.

"He's gone."

Darla put her hand over her mouth and sobbed violently. Moments later, Doug led Archie out of Travis' room. There were tears in Doug's eyes.

"Archie didn't want to leave Travis' side."

"I'll take him home with me now."

"Thanks, Darla."

Archie whimpered and kept looking back as Darla led him to her car. When Darla got home, the two dogs climbed into bed with her. She couldn't get Travis' words out of her mind—that God loved him and forgave him of all his sins.

What about my sin? I killed my baby. Could God ever forgive that?

Grateful that tomorrow was Saturday, she cried herself to sleep.

The next morning, Susie invited Darla to meet her for breakfast. Both women wore dark glasses as they sat down to eat.

"Darla, I'd like us to stay in touch."

"I'd like that."

"One thing I wanted to share with you—Travis died with a big smile on his face. I believe he told us the truth. He's in heaven now. He pleaded with me to ask Jesus into my heart so I would be with him in heaven. My brother Doug is a Christian. I never thought about it. I think I was angry with God for what Hank did to Travis. I also got too busy. Last night, I couldn't stop thinking about what Travis said. I have a meeting tomorrow with Pastor Brian."

"Travis asked me the same exact thing. I told him I'd think about it."

"We are having Travis' service next Saturday. He requested we have a closed casket. He wanted everyone to remember him alive. We are all going to share something about Travis. We would like for you to share too."

"Thank you. I would be honored to share."

The women parted with a hug. Darla went home and called Rayleen and Clayton to invite them to Travis' celebration of life.

"We are so sorry for your loss. We know he was a good friend to you. We'll be there to support you. How about if you bring Archie and Spanky over before to have a play day with Sunshine. I know Archie must be feeling the loss of his master."

"You got that right. He hasn't wanted to eat since Travis died. Archie started to howl the moment Travis died."

"I've heard dogs can sense when a spirit is leaving a body."

Darla wanted to tell her closest friends about Travis' final request. At the moment, it was much too personal. She still needed time to process it.

Friday night before Travis' service, there was a knock on Darla's door.

Who could this be? Clayton's not picking up the dogs until early morning.

When she opened the door, Susie stood there with a big box in her hand.

"Hi, Susie."

"Sorry to not call first. I decided just to drop by to see if you were home."

"Sure. Come in."

"Darla, I brought over some things that belonged to Travis. I think he would have wanted you to have. Also, Archie's toys, bowls, and dog food."

"Are you sure? What about you and your other siblings?"

"We took what we wanted."

"These items I think are special to you and Travis."

Darla opened the box. First Susie took out his 'Life is Golden' sweatshirt. Next, she handed Darla his Iowa jacket.

"He said you liked this jacket. You said it made him look like a farm boy."

Darla laughed. She remembered saying that. Susie took a small cross on a chain out of the box.

"I have no idea where he got this. But this is the one thing he insisted we give you."

Tears once again formed in Darla's eyes.

"Here's one more thing I think will mean a lot to you."

She placed a journal in Darla's hand.

"I only read a few pages—it's mostly about you."

A look of surprise spread over Darla's face as her eyes widened.

Travis wrote about me in his journal? It's going to be awhile until I can read this.

"Thanks, Susie."

"You're welcome. And thanks for being such a good friend to my brother. See you tomorrow."

That night, when the nightmares came, Darla decided she would try to pray. Ashamed of herself, she had distanced herself from God and felt unworthy. Darla cried out, "God, if you're there, I need help. I can't handle this anymore."

36

Travis's funeral was held on December 15. That morning, Darla had to put an ice pack on her eyes to bring down the swelling. Later, as she entered the church, Susie motioned her to the front. Darla made an effort not to look at the casket. Travis' siblings shared about their life with Travis. Susie was the last to give tribute to her brother. When Darla's turn came, she was grateful she hadn't prepared anything. She wanted to speak from her heart.

"When Travis and I became friends, I was going through one of the hardest times of my life. He listened and encouraged me to look for the good in everything that happens to us. His favorite song was 'Hey Jude.' He loved the line: *take a sad song and make it better*.

"Travis once told me that someday he wanted to write a book similar to the book *All I Really Needed to Know I Learned in Kindergarten*. Instead, he wanted to name his book *All I Need to Know How to Live I Learned From My Dog*.

"He loved his golden retriever Archie and Archie loved

him. From Archie he learned love, loyalty, and to give not expecting anything in return. Travis knew what it meant to be a friend." Darla looked down at Travis' casket.

"I love you Travis and will never forget you. Travis is not there."

She pointed to the casket. "He's in heaven now."

Darla walked off the platform and sat down.

Pastor Brian spoke next. "Darla, thank you. You are right. Travis has gone to his heavenly home, no more pain and no more tears. Right before Travis passed, he made the most important decision of his life. He asked Jesus to come into his life. He begged me to share the salvation message with you. No matter what a mess you've made of your life, no matter what terrible things you've done, Jesus will forgive you. However broken you are, he'll put your life back together. Jesus is waiting with open arms. He loves you. If you'd like to give your life to Jesus, please come forward."

This is what I need. I think Jesus can help me fix my broken life. I need to surrender.

Darla practically ran to the altar. Tears rolling down her cheeks. As she lifted her hand to wipe them away, she noticed Susie and several others standing there too.

The pastor turned to those who came forward. "Pray this prayer after me: 'Jesus, I know I am a sinner, I ask for your forgiveness. I believe you died for my sins and rose from the dead. I ask you to come into my heart and life. I want to trust and follow you as my Lord and Savior.'"

Immediately after Darla prayed, she felt a load lifted from her shoulders. She turned to Susie.

They fell into each other's arms. Pastor Brian led them back to their seats.

He whispered, "I'd like to invite you two ladies to church tomorrow."

"We'll be there, pastor," they echoed together.

She knew they could accept the pastor's invitation to church since she didn't need to take Susie to the airport until early evening.

At the cemetery, Darla couldn't cry. Instead, she said a silent prayer.

Thank you, God for putting it on Travis' heart to share the truth with me.

All of a sudden, she saw an image of Travis as a young boy—powerless and vulnerable—desperately trying to protect his little sister. Then she saw a vision of him as a shattered man trying to deal with the effects of the trauma—scared, alone, ashamed, plagued by nightmares and flashbacks. Worse yet, relationships were dangerous, and intimacy was impossible. Suddenly, she was enveloped by a glorious peace. She saw Travis in heaven surrounded by unconditional love. His identity no longer shaped by the sexual assault. She saw Jesus holding Travis in his arms like a loving father—accepted and free. Darla was certain Travis now experienced the freedom he so longed for.

The next morning, Darla picked Susie up for church. Pastor Brian greeted the people as they came in.

He approached Darla and Susie. "Please stay a few

minutes after the service. I have something I'd like to give to you two."

Darla loved the service. She sang along with the words displayed on the screen for the worship songs. The message touched her. Pastor Brian spoke on forgiveness—forgiveness is a choice—letting go of anger, resentment, and bitterness to someone who has wronged you. It's not about excusing their actions but about choosing to release the negative emotions it has caused.

That's what I need to do. I've been holding on to all this anger and bitterness against Jesse and Giani. It's not hurting them. They've moved on with their lives. It's hurting me.

She and Susie waited as Pastor Brian requested. About fifteen minutes later, Pastor Brian walked over and handed each woman a Bible.

"This is to help you with your spiritual growth. Begin reading in the book of John. You take care of yourself, Susie. I'll be praying for you."

"Thanks, pastor."

Pastor Brian hugged them both.

"You want to go out to lunch, Susie?" Darla asked.

"Sure. I'm practically packed. We don't have to leave for the airport until 4:30 p.m."

At lunch, Darla said, "I think God brought Travis into my life to bring me to the decision I made today asking Jesus into my heart."

"Most definitely, Darla. We didn't really grow up with any religion. Our parents took us to church at Easter and Christmas. Travis was more curious about God than I was.

The peace I saw Travis experience when he accepted Christ made me want it too."

"You're right, Susie, this isn't a religion. It's more of a relationship with a God who loved us so much that he sent his only son to die for us. I need to share this with all my friends. Let's stay in touch. We can share what we learn from reading the Bible Pastor Brian gave us."

Susie hugged Darla at the airport. "I feel like I have sister. I see what my brother saw in you."

Darla smiled and waved as Susie walked to her gate.

Darla phoned Rayleen when she got home. "I'm back from the airport. Can Clayton bring the dogs home?"

"Of course. Good news—we crumbled up some chicken training treats in the dog food and Archie ate some."

"That's great."

Spanky and Archie were so excited to see Darla. They both jumped up and licked her face as they wagged their tails.

"Good boys. I missed you too." Although Darla was tired from the long day, she took out the Bible and read the inscription in the front.

Darla, this is a love letter from God. Use this book as a guidebook for your life. Blessings, – PASTOR BRIAN

She set her alarm, climbed into bed, and reached again for her Bible. She started reading in the book of John and fell asleep.

The next morning when the alarm went off, she couldn't find Archie. She found him in the living room. He had pulled Travis' sweatshirt out of the box and was sleeping on it. Her eyes welled up.

"I miss him too, boy."

She decided to let him sleep on the shirt.

This is the first Christmas in a long time I feel hope and peace instead of regret and heartbreak.

❧ 37 ❧

March 1981

It didn't take Darla's associates long to see the change in Darla. Rayleen and Clayton were the first to ask her about it. Darla wore a smile consistently. Her disposition was positive and even her posture changed. During the ordeal with Giani, she slumped over when she walked.

When she walked now, she stood straight with confidence.

After she shared about how she had asked Jesus into her life and received the gift of salvation with Clayton and Rayleen, they watched the peace in Darla's life. They agreed to attend church with her. With the change in Darla together with the messages delivered by Pastor Brian, it took only three weeks for Clayton and Rayleen to accept Jesus as their savior. Only two weeks later, Rayleen discovered they were expecting their first child. Clayton told Darla after church that Sunday, "It's so timely that we just gave our lives to Christ. We will raise our child as a Christian."

Darla was feeling more joy and peace now. She continued to grow in her knowledge of the Bible, and she got involved in a women's Bible study. Darla and the leader of the study became instant friends. Fawn, a middle-aged woman, was passionate to see women healed and whole. Fawn also taught literature at San Diego State. She wasn't just brilliant but beautiful with flowing black hair, sky blue eyes, and a captivating smile.

When she heard Darla's testimony, she encouraged Darla to share her story.

"Darla, the things we go through are not for us. They're for the people we can help. Truly, your newfound relationship with Christ has made you an overcomer. You've learned to let go of the pain and brokenness and forgive those who hurt you. I think we could work together to put together a little booklet of Scriptures to help women who are going through the things you went through. One Scripture we could use is Galatians 5:1 in the Amplified Bible: 'It was for this freedom that Christ set us free; therefore keep standing firm and do not be subject again to a yoke of slavery.'"

"Do you really think we could do that, Fawn?"

"Of course. You can do all things through Christ. I'll help you."

"You know I could contact one of the publishers who worked with Travis to help us with it."

Once Darla and Fawn started writing, they became more and more excited. Joe Mueller, one of Travis' associates and friends, offered to publish her book. He even helped choose the title: *You're not Humpty Dumpty—God CAN put the broken pieces of your life back together.*

The booklet was published six months later on November 2, 1981. Working together with Fawn and researching Scriptures helped Darla grow closer to God.

Everyone at Darla's office supported her and purchased a copy of her booklet. One morning, Shirley, her boss, called Darla into her office.

"I am so proud of you for having the courage to share your story. I can see your passion for helping women. I want you to know you have helped me."

Darla moved closer to the end of her chair looking questionably at Shirley. Shirley continued, "My husband and I haven't thought much about God in a long time. I guess we just got busy with life. I talked to him after reading your booklet about making God a priority again. He agreed. Thank you, Darla."

Darla smiled.

"That's not all I wanted to speak to you about."

Darla's eyebrow went up.

"I have a friend and colleague, Jim Anderson. Dr. Anderson and I attended college together and after graduation worked at the same clinic. Recently, he opened a Christian Counseling Center here in San Diego. The center has grown. He needs to hire another counselor to start in about four months. He contacted me to see if I knew anyone who might be interested in working there. Of course, I instantly thought of you. I hate losing you. I think you would be a perfect fit for his counseling center. It would be a slight reduction in your salary. I think you could handle that. There would always be opportunity for advancement. What do you think?"

"I think it sounds wonderful. Now that I'm a Christian, I love to counsel using the Bible."

"You certainly will be able to do that. I will arrange a meeting as soon as possible with Dr. Anderson."

Darla thanked Shirley. She barely could contain her excitement.

This is what I prayed for. Thank you, God.

38

November 1981

The Monday after Thanksgiving, she met Jim Anderson for lunch. Shirley told her to take her time and not to worry about heading back to the office. Jim was a pleasant-looking man with a strong handshake. His brown hair was graying at the temples. He was tall with compassionate green eyes. He spoke with confidence about his endeavors at the clinic.

"We want to help people sharing God's perspective on their issues. All our counseling is based on the Pauline Epistles. If you decide to come on board, you will be required to take some additional training. California Graduate School of Theology sends their instructors to San Diego to train our counselors using the Pauline Epistles. When you complete this training, you will earn a certificate in biblical counseling. This training will take place two evenings a week for four weeks. This is quite a commitment—it will be more than worth it in the end. Well, Darla, are you interested?"

"Absolutely. This is an answer to my prayer. I couldn't be more grateful for the opportunity to work with you."

Dr. Anderson stood up, smiled, and shook her hand. "Welcome to our team, Darla."

"Thank you, Dr. Anderson."

The first week of March, Darla started working at Dr. Jim Anderson's Christian Counseling Center and taking biblical counseling classes. Although it was a little tiring to work all day and then go to classes, she loved every minute of it. Rayleen cut her hours since she was progressing in her pregnancy. She offered to help Darla out with the dogs.

"Thank you. It helped me immensely as I did the research."

So proud to be working at a Christian Counseling Center, she called Amy to share the good news with her.

"Wow, Darla. How amazing. I'm so happy for you. I was just going to call you myself. I have some exciting news too. I just found out yesterday that I'm pregnant."

"Congratulations, dear friend. I know you and Steven are so happy."

"I'm going to have a little girl. Will you honor me and be her godmother?"

"Absolutely. Have you chosen a name yet?"

"Probably Noel. My due date is December twenty-fourth. One more bit of news. Steven and I read the booklet you wrote. We loved it. Steven was brought up as a

Christian. He kind of walked away from his faith in college. We both gave our life to Christ and now attend church every week. We love our church."

"That's wonderful news. Rayleen is due in November. She, too, is having a girl. Looks like I'm going to be an aunt to two little girls."

Even though I'm happy for my friends, I can't help but feel sad. I don't know if it's envy or grief or both.

Darla felt a huge knot in her stomach. A tear slid down her cheek.

In spite of her ongoing struggle with the past, Darla experienced a peace in her heart knowing her two closest friends were now walking with Jesus.

It's all because of Travis, my dear friend. All these people will be in heaven thanks to him.

Darla loved her counseling job, although she missed working alongside Rayleen and Clayton. She believed she was right where God wanted her. She not only helped people, but she could use the Bible to do that.

After Darla had worked at the Christian Counseling Center for three months, Dr. Anderson approached her as she was preparing to go home.

"Darla, do you have a minute? I'd like to talk to you about something important."

"Of course."

"My church is planning a mission trip to Ejido Urua-pan, Mexico at the end of the month. We will be bringing a team of men to build an orphanage. Medical and dental professionals will accompany us. Also, a group of women will come to minister to children and teach them English. I think you would be a good fit for this mission project. We would leave on a Friday after work and return the following Sunday. What do you think? Is this something that would interest you?"

"It sounds like an amazing opportunity. Of course, I need to pray about it. I'd have to make arrangements for my dogs. What about work?"

"Yes. I definitely would want you to pray about this. As far as work, I think the other counselors can handle things the five workdays we'll be gone."

That evening, Darla accepted an invitation to dinner at Clayton and Rayleen's. After dinner, she shared Dr. Anderson's proposal to join his church on a mission trip to Mexico.

Clayton spoke up first, "Wow, Darla, what a chance for you to help these children."

Rayleen chimed in, "You would be great at this. Don't concern yourself with Spanky and Archie. Sunshine loves them. They are part of our family. Now that I'm only working part-time they'll keep me company."

That night, Darla prayed about whether she should go to Mexico. She picked up her Bible to read before she fell asleep and right away it opened to the Scripture in Mark 16:15: *Go into all the world and preach the gospel to all creation.*

The Scripture resonated in her mind as she slept.

The next morning, she woke up with a perfect peace about joining Dr. Anderson and his church on the mission trip. She almost flew into Dr. Anderson's office when she arrived at work.

"I'm going," Darla announced looking directly at Dr. Anderson with a wide smile and eyes bright and shining.

"That's wonderful. I know you will be an asset to the other women going. We have been saved to serve others."

"Do you know the ages of the children we will be ministering to? I'd like to buy some small toys, hair bows, coloring books, and any other things they may like."

"Hey, that's a great idea. I'll try to find out their ages."

The next few weeks, Darla's thoughts were consumed with going to Mexico. Every free moment she ran around buying gifts for the children. At a meeting with Carol, Jim Anderson's wife, and the other six women going on the mission trip, she found out the ages of the children ranged from four to fourteen. Carol and Darla went on a shopping trip for the children. At a Christian bookstore, they found cute finger puppets and big books to teach Bible stories. At the 99 Cents Only store, they purchased match box cars, coloring books, hair bows, and candy bars for the older children.

❧ 39 ❧

July 1982

After work on Friday, Jim and Carol picked Darla up to leave on the mission trip. They didn't want her to leave her car at the church. Before they left, the pastor prayed over each of them for traveling mercies. The four church vans and six cars of people loaded up. Darla glanced at the men getting in the van with Jim and noticed that one of them looked slightly familiar, but she couldn't figure out why. Darla and Carol rode in another van with the other women. On the ride down to Mexico, the group of women sang praise songs. Darla felt the joy of the Lord. Ever since Rayleen and Amy shared their news about expecting baby girls, Darla kind of felt left out. Her dream had been that their children would grow up together.

Now it's impossible. I'm not even married.

Darla knew what she needed to do—not let these negative thoughts take over her mind—trust God. Hadn't he taken care of her so far. Trust that he loved her uncondi-tionally and that he works all things for her good. Believe that he has a prefect plan for her life.

Matthew 6:33 became the Scripture verse she leaned on: *But first and most importantly seek his kingdom and his righ-teousness, and all these things will be given to you also.*

As she meditated on this promise, her entire thought pattern changed. Instead of focusing on the possibility of not having a child, she focused on being happy for her friends and praying for their easy delivery and healthy babies.

When they arrived at the church in Mexico, the excite-ment of the children greeting the women touched Darla's heart. The very first thing the women did was pass out the gifts to the children.

"Gracias! Muchas gracias!" the children echoed over and over.

Carol sat the women down.

"We have thirty-two children. Since there are eight of us, we will be responsible for four children each. I've put your groups together by close ages."

Darla's excitement grew. *Four children only. That will give me a chance to get close to these kids and love them.*

Carol assigned Darla children aged five and six. Her responsibility was for two girls and two boys—Enrique, José, Lucinda, and Maria. Each child was special in their own way. Enrique—a bundle of energy. José—a voice like an angel. Lucinda—smart and spoke English well. Maria—shy and withdrawn. Her large, sad, dark eyes resembled a Margaret Keene painting.

At the evening meeting with the other women, Carol handed Darla some file folders.

"Here are the files on the children you are responsible for. Once you see what they've been through, you'll have a better understanding on how to relate to them."

Later that evening, Darla sat quietly reading each child's file. The information given devastated her. She learned that Enrique's parents were brutally murdered while he was in his playpen. No one could handle him. He often would go into fits of rage—crying, screaming, and throwing things. His grandmother finally brought him to Hope Chapel, Pastor Tom Sepulveda's church.

Pastor Tom took Enrique in, and he and his wife Belinda have done all they could, his high energy level can be a problem.

José's parents were in a horrific car accident. His father recovered. His mother suffered severe brain damage. She passed away a year later. His father was never the same after that. He drank heavily and often neglected José. Finally, his uncle brought him to Pastor Sepulveda. Pastor Sepulveda discovered that José was blessed with an incredible singing voice.

Lucinda's mother, a victim of rape at sixteen, never was in a position to care for a child. Her grandmother raised her until she turned four. When her grandmother suffered from Dementia, a concerned neighbor alerted Pastor Sepulveda of the situation. He went and got Lucinda a year and a half ago. Belinda, his wife, let her sit in as she home schooled her own children. That's where she picked up her understanding of English.

Maria's background broke Darla's heart. One afternoon, when Pastor Sepulveda passed through the worst slums of the city, he found Maria sitting by a dumpster. She sat holding a dead cat gnawing on a bone. Her hair matted, her body filthy, and her clothes practically in rags.

Apparently abandoned, Pastor Sepulveda went to her. It took him thirty minutes to coax her into his car. Full of fear, she didn't speak for three days. Belinda cried at the condition of the little girl. She won her trust by giving her chocolate bars. Once she got her cleaned up, Belinda wanted a doctor to examine her. Thankfully she hadn't been violated. It took Belinda several days and an entire bottle of detangler to get the mats out of Maria's hair. Darla's face was covered with tears when she finished reading Maria's history. She got on her knees and prayed:

Lord, thank you for sending me here to help these children. Help me to share your love with them. Let my hands be your hands.

Darla's parents had donated two thousand dollars to help with the building materials for the orphanage. They also gave Darla three hundred dollars to purchase gifts for the children. Darla still had some of these gifts in her suitcase. The next morning, she brought the presents to the children. To Enrique she gave a superhero backpack, a toy John Deere truck, and several rolls of flavored candies. To José she gave a Willy Coyote backpack, a dump truck, and flavored candies. Lucinda received a Hello Kitty purse, a stuffed teddy bear, and a package of chuckles. Darla presented Maria with a Hello Kitty purse too.

When she handed Maria a baby doll, Maria took the doll and held it like a real baby and said, "Go to sleep, baby Rosie. You're safe now."

Tears welled up in Darla's eyes. Watching Lucinda take a bite of each colored chuckle and then put it back in the package brought a grin to her face.

To make the children feel comfortable with her, she brought an interactive game to teach them how to have fun. It blessed her heart to watch the children giggling, falling, and enjoying themselves.

Next, she taught the children the song *Jesus Loves Me* along with the sign language to go along with it.

José stepped forward. "Miss Darla, Miss Darla, I sing in my language?"

"Yes. Go ahead. Teach us the words."

José sang his heart out. *Truly this little boy has been blessed with a gift from God. He sings like an angel.*

The other children joined in with José. They learned fast.

"Children, let's take turns singing first in Spanish and then we'll sing it in English."

After singing each ten times, Darla struggled to get the children to stop. It took her standing up and demonstrating a marching hand gesture song called "Father Abraham". The children finally quit to do something else. Darla suddenly realized she'd need to move more quickly on the new activities. Next, Darla pulled out the finger puppets to tell them the salvation message using puppetry, The children loved this activity. That evening, the workers ate with the children. The men grilled hot dogs and hamburgers. The people from the church baked cookies. Pastor Sepulveda's wife Belinda taught the children how to make s'mores.

Before Darla turned in for the night, Carol told her, "The doctor will be examining the children tomorrow. So be aware there will be an interruption in your schedule. Also, the youth groups here at Hope Chapel put together a short evangelistic skit to share with your group tomorrow. They should be here first thing in the morning."

The next morning, Darla gathered the four children together. Maria ran up, hugged Darla, and said, "Te quiro mucho."

Darla smiled and hugged her back. She knew it meant I really love you.

Darla repeated the words, "Te quiro mucho."

The children all giggled.

"Why are you all laughing?"

José spoke up, "Miss Darla, you sound funny trying to talk Mexican."

The youth group showed up at that time. The skit they performed was not only age appropriate for five-and six-year-olds, but the message was so powerful. The children didn't squirm at all during the twenty-five-minute performance. Even Enrique sat mesmerized. They portrayed a mean child who stole and bullied other children—representing sin. Then he saw Jesus on the cross taking the punishment the child deserved for his sins. Last, it depicted Jesus welcoming the child into heaven. The skit affected Maria with such emotion she began to cry.

After the performance, Darla gave each child a Scripture card with the Scripture John 3:16. Next she showed them large chocolate bars.

"When you memorize this Scripture, you will earn one of these bars."

Lucinda shouted out, "I'm going to be the first to memorize it."

Just then the medical assistant walked into the classroom.

"Dr. Terry is ready for the children now. Would you please follow me into the clinic."

"Sure. Come on children."

On the way, his assistant asked Darla to help reassure the children that it was going to be all right during their examinations. When they walked into the clinic, Dr. Terry smiled. He walked up and extended his hand to Darla. "Hello, I'm Michael Terry. Thank you for helping out."

Darla recognized his nice smile as the man she noticed when they were loading the vans. She smiled back. "You're very welcome. I'm blessed to be here. I consider it a privilege to help these children."

Dr. Terry turned to the children. "Hi, kids. I'm Dr. Terry."

He put on a funny red nose. The children laughed.

"What are your names?"

One by one they yelled out their names. "I have this cool treasure chest. If you earn a star today, you get to choose three things from my treasure chest."

Lucinda raised her hand.

"Yes, young lady."

"How do you get a star?"

"I have to look in your ears, check your eyes, and check your bones and blood. If you do a good job letting me check you out, you'll get a star and get to go into the treasure chest."

"I'll be good," Enrique shouted.

Darla held Maria's hand during all the exams. When it came time to draw blood, Dr. Terry told the children to keep their eyes on the picture of the clown on the wall.

"See if you can guess how many polka dots are on his hat. Whoever's guess is closest to the right answer wins a giant lollipop."

Darla also helped distract the children while Dr. Terry drew blood. Enrique won. He guessed fifty. The correct answer was fifty-five. All four of the children earned a star and got to pick three things from the treasure chest. The children thought the whole experience was fun. José asked, "Dr. Terry, can we come back to see you tomorrow?"

"No José. But can I come and visit you and your teacher sometime?"

All together the children shouted, "Yes."

40

By the time they returned to the classroom, it was lunch time for the children. Darla escorted them to the area designated as a lunchroom. The ladies from Hope Chapel made peanut butter and jelly and bologna sandwiches, along with apples and cookies for the children.

Darla went into the lounge for the adults. She really needed a coffee. Today for lunch the women prepared Cobb salads for the workers.

Dr. Terry walked in with his assistant. He glanced over at Darla, smiled, and waved. She nodded and smiled back. Out of the corner of her eye she took another look at Michael Terry. Suddenly it occurred to her that he reminded her of Clancy from the movie "The Man from Snowy River"—tough yet gentle.

Darla quickly shifted her eyes away from him when she noticed him walking toward her.

"Hi. How's the salad?" Dr. Terry asked.

"It's good."

"I see you're drinking coffee. I'm glad our team brought

cases of water. You've got to be careful of the water here. Oh, please excuse me. Earlier I told you my name, but I didn't ask for yours."

"It's Darla. Darla Greystone."

"It's a pleasure to meet you, Miss Greystone."

"Darla please." Then she looked at him in disbelief. *He's the first person who didn't respond, "Darla from* Our Gang.*"*

What a kind man this Michael Terry is. He's so good with the children.

"I hope you have an awesome day, Darla."

Darla returned to her classroom as the children filed in. Maria, as usual, got as close as she could to Darla on the floor. She even held on to Darla's leg. This little girl had more than captured Darla's heart.

She took out the big book she used to tell the Bible stories from. Next to it she placed a flannel board. The children participated in the stories putting felt figures on the flannel board that related to the story. She began to tell them the story of Daniel in the lion's den. It was Enrique's turn to place the figures on the flannel board. Each time he put a lion on the board, he made growling sounds. The children howled with laughter.

When the days lessons were over, Maria hesitated and did not leave with the other children.

Instead, she climbed up on Darla's lap. Gently, she stroked Darla's cheek.

"Pretty." She touched Darla's hair. "Soft."

Snuggling into Darla, she looked up with her dark sad eyes.

"Will you be my mother, Miss Darla?"

Surprised and saddened, Darla gasped, not knowing how to respond. She just held the little girl. "You are such a sweet little girl. I love you too."

Darla took Maria by the hand and walked her out. Tears welled up in her eyes. Maria looked up at Darla again. Darla patted her head.

"Go play with the other children, Maria."

Darla wiped her eyes. She hurried to escape to her room. Running past Carol, Carol grabbed her arm. "Is everything all right, Darla?"

Darla mumbled, "I just need some time alone."

She fell on her bed when she got into the room. Uncontrollable tears fell on her pillow. The door opened. Carol sat down on her bed.

She put her hand on Darla's back. "I know this is hard. These children grip your heart. We do the best we can sharing Jesus and his love with them. We will never be able to fix their lives or undo their past."

Carol's right. We can't undo their pasts. Just like I can't undo mine. I know God's forgiven me for murdering my baby. I'm still carrying my hidden secret. What would others think if they knew?

Darla sat up. "I get that. But it's different with Maria. There's a bond there that I can't explain. She asked me to be her mother."

"Wow, I see. Maria is a needy child. She longs to have parents. Sometimes I think she still has a memory somewhere of a mother. That is what's driving this need in her. Just watch how she reacts with the baby doll you gave her.

She perfectly mimics a mother with a child. Maria needs lots of prayer. Let's prayer for her right now."

Darla took Carol's hands. Both women bowed their heads and prayed.

The next day, Lucinda rushed into the classroom shouting, "I got this. I got this."

Darla grabbed her shoulders. "Got what?"

"Johnny 3:16. I know it."

Darla chuckled. "Okay Lucinda, once we all sit down and say our morning prayer, you can go first." After prayer time, Lucinda recited John 3:16 perfectly. She jumped up and down when Darla handed her the giant chocolate bar. A wide smile formed across her face. Then she glanced at the other three children.

Looking up at Darla, she asked, "May I share this with my friends?"

Her generosity touched Darla's heart.

"Of course, sweetheart."

The sad faces of the other children instantly changed to smiles.

On the following day, when the others recited their scripture memory verse, they followed Lucinda's example and shared their prize chocolate bar.

The day before the scheduled day for the group to return home, Darla helped the children create a wordless book. They learned that each colored page had a special meaning: black symbolized SIN Romans 3:23, red BLOOD John 3:16, white WHITE AS SNOW Psalm 21:18, gold HEAVEN—STREETS OF GOLD Revelation 21:18, green GROWING PLANTS 2 Peter 3:18. They learned that plants need three things to grow—sunshine, rain, and good soil. Christians need three things to grow in Jesus—praying, reading the Bible, and spending time with other believers.

Just as they were finishing up their books, in walked Dr. Michael Terry.

"Hi, Enrique, José, Lucinda, and Maria. What are you doing?"

Apparently, he knew the salvation message behind the book. He wanted the children to explain. He held up the same book Darla made.

"Enrique, what's the black color for?"

"All the bad things we do."

"What's the name for that?"

"Sin," shouted out Lucinda.

"You're absolutely right, Lucinda. Can you tell me about the red color."

"It's for Jesus' blood because he died on the cross for us."

"Right."

"José, what's the white page for?"

"It's snow. Jesus makes us clean and white like snow."

"Good job."

"Who can tell me what the gold page represents?"

Maria raised her hand.

"Yes, Maria."

"It's heaven. I want to go there. No tears there. Everyone's happy."

"That's right, no more sadness or tears."

Lucinda tugged at Dr. Terry's arm.

"Can I tell about the green? Green's my favorite color."

"Sure. Go ahead."

Lucinda stood up proudly. "Green because to grow plants they need sunshine, rain, and good soil. For us to grow as Christians, we must pray, read the Bible, and spend time with other Christians."

"You did such a good job, Lucinda. Are you children ready to be baptized tonight?"

"Yes," they shouted together. After dinner, Pastor Sepulveda planned a short sermon for them. He then gave an invitation to those who wanted to be baptized. All the children nodded their heads. Maria raised her hand.

"Yes, Maria."

"I'm getting baptized so I can go to heaven and see Jesus."

Both Dr. Terry and Darla smiled.

After the baptism, Carol planned a banana split party for the children.

When Dr. Terry said good-bye to the children, Maria ran up and whispered something in his ear.

He hugged her, smiled, and looked over at Darla. She shrugged her shoulders and shook her head.

Later that evening, Darla saw Dr. Terry. She walked up to him.

"Hi. I guess you're curious about what Maria whispered to me."

Darla nodded.

"She told me I really like you, Dr. Terry. Do you want to be my daddy?"

Darla's eyebrows furrowed.

"She asked me to be her mother."

Dr. Terry shook his head.

"Her story is so sad. All they know about her is what she told them—my name is Maria—no last name. The poor child was so traumatized when they found her. She's blocked everything out. No one knows how long she was on the street alone. Pastor Sepulveda told me he and his wife tried to ride her around to see if she could remember her home or anything. She just got on the floor in the back seat of the car crying and shouting, 'Don't leave me here.' After that, they didn't try again—just brought her back to the orphanage."

"No one ever came searching for her, Darla? No one contacted the police?"

"Never."

"She will miss you, Darla. I see how much she clings to you."

"Yes. I know that. I've promised to write letters to her every week. Pastor Sepulveda's wife, Belinda, will read them to her. I'm also going to send her and the other children things they may need."

"You're a good person, Darla. We were blessed to have you here to help."

The structure that would be used as the orphanage was almost finished thanks to the crew of men working almost around the clock.

Early the next morning, Carol gathered the women together for prayer. They prayed for the children they had worked with and for safe travels home.

"Today is not only going to be a hard day for all of you. Remember it's going to be even harder for the children.

They have connected with you like family. Many of them will cry. I have made cards for you to give to each of the children you've worked with. I've pasted a picture of you in it for them."

She handed out the cards. Every woman received a folder with a picture of herself with her group. Each child had signed their name.

They loaded the vans. The workers hugged and said goodbye to their children. Darla saved Maria to the last. Maria held on with all her might.

"Don't leave me, Miss Darla. Please don't leave me," she cried.

Darla's body went numb. A torrent of tears escaped down her cheeks. Pastor Sepulveda picked Maria up and cuddled her. No one spoke much on the drive home. Carol stroked Darla's hand. "I know it hurts now. Each day, it will get a little easier. Focus on the good you did for the children."

Darla returned home to her life and her schedule. She missed Maria. Maria had become part of her life. Her heart felt like it was pulled out of her. The separation added to the aching in her heart over her decision to abort her child.

As she promised, she wrote weekly to Maria and always included an individual message for each of the other children. She shopped relentlessly for the four children. She put extra thought into shopping for Maria. Her gifts needed to be special.

❧ 41 ❧

November 1982

Days turned into weeks and weeks turned into months. Amy and Rayleen's babies were due soon. Both women kept busy preparing for the arrival of their first baby.

Darla decided for Thanksgiving this year she would volunteer at the homeless shelter with her church. Darla and the other women decorated each table with pinecone turkeys the local school children made. Each table was covered with red, yellow, or orange tablecloths.

When the food was ready, the people filed in. Darla's job was scooping out mashed potatoes and sweet potatoes to put on each plate. Darla smiled at each person she served. She noticed a little girl with big dark eyes clinging to her mother. Her heart stopped. Her mind drifted back to Mexico to the little girl she left behind. She shook herself getting back to reality. After everyone was served, the workers fixed themselves a plate, and the pastor told them to mingle and sit among the people. Darla noticed an empty seat at the table with the dark-eyed girl and her mother.

"May I sit here with you? My name is Darla."

"We would like that," answered the mother.

Darla found out the little girl's name was Mary Ann, and her mother was Ruth. The child's father ran off and left them. The mother recently lost her job. They'd been living in their car. Darla excused herself and went to her purse. She had a one hundred-dollar bill and a little bracelet in it she planned to send to Maria. She returned to her seat. Taking the little box with the bracelet, she handed it to Mary Ann. The little girl's eyes grew big as she opened the box. Her hand flew to her mouth as she looked in the box.

"For me?"

"Yes. For you because you are such a sweet little girl."

"Put it on me, please, Mama."

Ruth reached over and placed the bracelet on her daughter's wrist. Ruth eyes glisten as she smiled at Darla.

"Thank you."

"You're welcome. This is for you, Ruth."

She put the hundred-dollar bill in Ruth's hand. Her eyes squinted as she looked questionably at Darla. Her eyes filled with tears.

"Ruth, I'd like to try to help you and Mary Ann. Please take my phone number. I'm a counselor. I may find some resources to help you."

"Thank you, Darla. I don't know what to say. You are so kind."

Ruth and Mary Ann got up to leave. Mary Ann hugged

Darla. She felt the same emotions she'd witnessed with Maria.

After they left, Darla sat thinking about the two little girls Maria and Mary Ann—two girls in two different places—just wanting love. All of a sudden, someone touched her shoulder. Turning her head she saw standing right before her Dr. Michael Terry. He just stood there staring at her.

"Hello, Michael."

Oh my! It's Dr. Terry. I never expected to see him again.

"Darla, it's great to see you. Since my parents are serving in the mission field, I like to come here and serve others instead of being alone. I just watched what you did. I've never known anyone as caring as you."

"My heart just goes out to these children."

"I saw you give that woman your phone number."

"Yes, I did. I'd love to get them some help—a place to stay until they get back on their feet."

"I may be able to assist you with that. Want to get some coffee after we're done here. I'll share what I have in mind."

"I'd like that. I got a ride here with Anna from our church. I'll let her know I don't need a ride home."

Michael and Darla cleaned up alongside the other workers. When they were finished, Michael took Darla by the arm and led her to his car. He took her to a quaint little coffee shop.

"I come here often. They have the best homemade blueberry muffins. It's a peaceful atmosphere."

Michael sat across from Darla. He smiled and stared intently at her.

Yes, he does resemble the physical character actor Clancy in "The Man from Snowy River."—a self-made man, tough guy, fearless. There's a calm serene inner strength about this man.

Michael spoke first, "So you gave that woman your phone number. It's your intention to try and help them?"

"Yes. She told me her husband left them. Recently, she's lost her job. Now they're sleeping in her car."

"I may be able to help. I'm not sure if you know, I'm a pediatrician with my own practice. One of my patients' grandmothers owns a large home. She takes in women who are pregnant with no resources but want to keep their babies. I could see if she has room for the woman and her child until they can get on their feet."

"Thanks, Michael. I really appreciate that."

"I'll phone her tomorrow and then maybe you'll agree to have dinner with me so I can let you know what she says." Darla blushed. Then she laughed.

"Never has anyone asked me out on a date like that before."

"Is it a date?"

They both chuckled softly.

"Yes. I would love to have dinner with you."

They sat in the coffee shop until it closed. Michael easily opened up about himself. His father was Australian. His mother was Irish. They met when his dad traveled to the United States after college. His parents now served as medical missionaries. Michael attended USC for medical school and finished his residency in San Diego.

"I got married while in college. My wife Rachael got

pregnant shortly after. She developed a brain tumor in her fourth month. When she slipped into a coma, they tried to save our baby. I lost them both."

Darla listened with compassion. She leaned forward and placed her hand on his. A single tear slid down her cheek.

"I'm so sorry, Michael." He put his head down. Darla left her hand on his.

"I never got angry with God or bitter. I guess that's why I went into pediatrics. Every child I help, I feel like it's my own."

Darla finally moved her hand. She moved closer to him and looked deeply into his eyes.

"I saw how tender you were with the children at the orphanage. You are definitely in the right field."

"Tell me about you, Darla."

Darla began, "I was married once for not too long. I found out he was already married to someone else."

"Oh my, Darla, I am so sorry someone did that to you."

Michael put his hand on her shoulder.

Just then the coffee shop attendant came over.

"Sorry folks, we're closing."

Thank you, God. I did not want to share anymore of my story. I can't believe I've opened up to this man so quickly. He makes me feel so comfortable. I'm so sad for what he went through, yet I admire his wanting to be a doctor and help children.

Michael walked Darla to the front door when they arrived at her house.

He extended his hand. "Thank you for having coffee with me. I hope I didn't bore you talking too much."

"Not at all."

"I'll pick you up at six o'clock for dinner. May I get your phone number just in case something comes up?"

She wrote down her phone number and handed it to him.

"Thank you. I look forward to seeing you again, Darla."

"Me too, Michael."

The next night, Darla had just returned from walking the dogs after work when her phone rang.

"Hello."

"Hello, Darla," Michael said. "I'm running a little behind with my patients. I may be thirty to forty minutes late. I hope that won't inconvenience you."

"No problem. Thank you for letting me know."

He sure is polite and courteous.

She no sooner hung up when her phone rang again.

"Hello."

"Hello, Darla. This is Ruth. My little girl and I met you yesterday. You gave me your number."

"Yes, Ruth. Of course, I remember you." She didn't want to get Ruth's hopes up so she didn't mention any details about how Michael might be able to help. "I'm working on it. Ruth, can you call me again tomorrow."

She gave Ruth her work number too.

"Thank you, Darla"

Darla dressed and waited for Michael, anxious to hear what he found out. He arrived at six thirty and apologized for being late. After he helped Darla into the car, he looked over at her.

"You look very pretty."

"Thank you. You look nice." They both laughed.

"Do you like dark chocolate?"

"What woman doesn't like chocolate?"

"The reason I'm asking you is I'm taking you to a fondue restaurant in the gaslight district. They have the best chocolate fondue dessert. You can dip pieces of cake and fruit in it."

"Sounds yummy."

After they ordered, Michael reached over and put his hand on her arm.

A big smile appeared on his face. "Darla, I've got great news for you. I checked with Sally today, the lady with the big house. Her exact words were, 'I'd be delighted to have them.' She also said she has some ideas of work for Ruth."

Darla reached over and hugged Michael. He pulled back, looking surprised for a moment. Then he hugged her back.

"Ruth called me right before you picked me up, Michael. I didn't say anything to her about this. I simply told her to get back to me tomorrow."

"I have an idea. Why not invite her over on Saturday? Then, Darla, both of us can take her over to Sally's house."

"Sounds great. I even have a better idea, Michael. I've planned on giving her some money to get her hair done and buy a few items of clothing. Why don't we ask her if we can watch Mary Ann while she does all that?"

"Even better, we could take Mary Ann to Walmart and get her some new clothes and let her pick out some toys. I want to chip in for this," Michael said.

Michael may resemble Clancy physically, but he is the ultimate gentle man—tender and kind. He exemplifies the kindness God shows toward us.

42

One evening before Saturday, Michael took Darla over to meet Sally. She was a round, cheerful German woman. Sally immediately scooped Darla up in her large arms.

"So glad to meet a friend of Dr. Terry's. Now you two come and have some of my apple strudel." She took Darla by the hand and led her to the kitchen. Michael smiled and shrugged his shoulders.

"Sally, this is delicious. Is this your own recipe?" Darla asked.

"It came from my great-grandmother back in the old country."

When they finished their coffee and strudel, Sally showed then the room she was going to let Ruth and Mary Ann use.

"I thought this would be good for a mother and child. I use it as my attic sewing room. There's a full and twin bed with more room for the little girl to play."

Darla noticed it even had a small bathroom with a toilet and sink.

"This is perfect, Sally. You are really blessing them."

"I also have some cute bedspreads and stuffed animals I'll put on their beds."

"Thank you."

Darla hugged Michael when he dropped her off.

"I can't thank you enough for what you've done for Ruth and her daughter."

"My pleasure. See you Saturday."

Ruth and Mary Ann arrived early Saturday morning. Darla didn't mention anything about the surprise. Michael showed up a little later. "You didn't tell them yet, Darla?"

"No. I'll wait until we get to Sally's. That's when I'm going to give Ruth the money and ask if we can watch Mary Ann."

"Sounds good."

"Where are you taking us, Darla?" Ruth asked.

"It's a surprise."

Sally bounded toward the group, her round red cheeks displaying a smile.

"Hi. You must be Ruth." She grabbed Ruth's hands and shook them.

"And you, pretty little lady, what's your name?"

"Mary Ann."

"Mary Ann. What a nice name. Would you like to see your new room?"

"What? Wait. What's going on here?"

"Ruth, I'm Sally. This is my home. For as long as you and your little girl need it, it's your home too."

As Ruth listened, tears welled in her eyes and no words came out. Sally grabbed Ruth by the arm and took Mary Ann by the hand.

"Come on, ladies. We'll all go check out your room."

Ruth and Mary Ann returned with big smiles on their faces. Mary Ann carried one of the teddy bears Sally had put on her bed.

"Miss Sally said I could have this. I'm going to call him Theodore. That's the real name for Teddy."

"Did you arrange all this, Darla?"

"No. Actually, Dr. Terry did."

Ruth walked over and gave Michael a hug.

"Thank you so much."

Just then Sally walked back in.

"More good news."

"What?" Michael asked.

Sally said, "Looks like I have a job for you, Ruth."

Ruth's eyes widened in amazement. "A job?"

"Yes. How would you like to work as a teacher's aide in a first grade class?"

Unable to contain her excitement, Ruth threw her hands up and jumped up and down shouting, "Hallelujah!" Darla stepped forward. "Ruth, to celebrate your new job, Dr. Terry and I want to bless you."

She handed Ruth two crisp hundred-dollar bills. "This is for you to go get your hair done and get some new work clothes."

Surprise stole the air from Ruth's lungs, leaving her breathless.

"One more thing, Ruth. Michael and I would like to

take Mary Ann out for some ice cream and a special treat while you're getting your hair done and shopping."

"Wow. I am overwhelmed by your generosity, Darla and Dr. Terry. Thank you."

"Mary Ann, Miss Darla and Dr. Terry are going to watch you this afternoon. They have some wonderful things planned for you."

"Oh goody."

Darla and Michael took Mary Ann by the hand after she hugged her mother good-bye. First, they took her for ice cream. She ordered a hot fudge sundae with cherry vanilla ice cream, sprinkles, and whipped cream. Next stop Walmart. Mary Ann picked out two skirts, a blouse, sweater, and tennis shoes. In the toy section, they bought her a paint set, two coloring books, and a doll that came with a stroller.

When they returned to Sally's, Darla was astonished by the transformation of Ruth. Her hair now cut in long layers just above her shoulders. The hairdresser added an auburn color to her hair. It brought out the green in her eyes. Ruth clapped her hands together and cried happy tears when she saw her daughter twirling around in delight as she showed off her new things.

Michael and Darla excused themselves.

"What a splendid day, Darla."

"Right. I'm feeling wonderful that we could help Ruth and Mary Ann." Darla smiled as she walked to the car.

"How about some Mexican food?"

"I love Mexican."

Michael linked arms with Darla. Michael didn't say much as they drove to the restaurant.

The Mexican restaurant featured a Mariachi band. They played a song entitled "La Mano de Dios"—or God's Hand. They sang the song first in Spanish then in English. The lyrics talked about a love so strong that only God was able to break it apart. The song touched Darla's heart.

"Michael, listen to the words of this song. Imagine a love like that—only the hand of God could break it apart."

"That's the kind of love I had with my wife Rachael. Only death broke us apart."

"You were fortunate to have that kind of love."

"Only God can bring that kind of love into your life. Trust God, Darla. He has that for you."

Darla tilted her head and placed her hand on her cheek. She seriously considered what Michael said. Michael snapped her back to the moment.

"The best part of today was shopping with Mary Ann. Have you ever seen a little girl so thankful? I can still see her little face covered with whipped cream eating her hot fudge sundae."

Darla smiled. "Yes, it felt so good to bless that little girl. Yet it made me think about a little girl alone without parents back in Mexico."

"Maria—yes, I pray for her daily."

"I want to go visit her this summer, Michael."

"Maybe we can both go."

For a moment, neither spoke. The silence heavy with unspoken words. Darla felt her breath catch. She saw something in Michael's intense gaze—a vulnerability that mirrored her own.

He wants to go with me in the summer. So, is he saying we'll be together then?

Michael's eyes crinkled at the edges. The corners of his mouth turned upward. Soon he was grinning, and so was she. At that instant there was a knowing between the two of them—they were in a relationship.

❧ 43 ❧

December 1982

Rayleen and Clayton's baby girl had been born on November twenty-second. Darla became the godmother to Winter Hope. A month later, on December twenty-fifth, Amy and Steven's baby girl, Noel, came into the world. Darla flew back to New York for the celebration. Once again, she was given the role of godmother. Holding that precious baby girl in her arms, she thought of her own child whose life she ended.

Will I ever have my own baby in the future?

On the plane trip home, Darla's thoughts drifted back to Mexico. She thought about the gifts and the many relatives and friends celebrating her best friend's baby. Contrasting to the little girl never celebrated—only abandoned. She unconsciously wiped away tears.

Lord, somehow help me to save Maria.

Michael picked Darla up at the airport.

Michael ran up to her at the baggage claim. She fell into his arms.

"I've missed you, Darla."

"I've only been gone a week. Missed you too. I have lots of pictures to share with you." She decided not to share her thoughts of Maria with him.

Only happy thoughts—thanking God for healthy moms and babies.

As they climbed into Michael's car, he said, "I'm glad you decided to come home on New Year's Eve. I want to take you out for a special dinner. After that, my church is having a New Year's Eve service to usher in the new year. It starts at ten and goes until midnight."

"Thanks. I'm looking forward to a good meal. I'm famished." Michael dropped Darla off. He took care of Archie and Spanky for Darla while she was gone. He already dropped off the dogs before going to the airport.

"Pick you up at six."

Darla showered, loved on the dogs, and wrapped the present she had for Michael. While she was in New York, she found a gold cross she knew Michael would like.

I'll surprise him with it at dinner.

She laid down with the dogs for a two-hour nap.

Michael had the same idea. He decided to bring Darla's Christmas gift to dinner. He'd put a lot of thought into her gift.

Darla dressed in a red velvet dress she purchased while shopping in New York. The neckline slightly came off the shoulders. She wore a gold heart locket her mother gave her for graduation.

Putting her hair up on the sides with rhinestone barrettes, she smiled, pleased with what she saw in the mirror.

Michael arrived exactly at six o'clock. He wore black slacks, a light blue shirt, and a charcoal sports jacket. He handed Darla a bouquet of a dozen roses—six white and six red.

"Michael, these are beautiful."

Darla kissed him gently on the cheek. Michael grinned and pointed upward. Above him he'd fastened a mistletoe to the ceiling. Darla felt her face grow warm. She knew she was blushing.

Tenderly, he held her. His lips brushed hers. Darla held her breath. As gently as he held her, he released her. She looked up into his eyes—eyes that were a window to his heart.

I'm falling in love with Michael Terry, I think he's in love with me.

Michael interrupted her daydream.

"We better go. Got reservations for six forty-five."

"Where are we going?"

"It's a surprise."

"Darla, you looking stunning tonight," Michael said, as he helped her into her black fur jacket.

"And you, Dr. Terry, are quite handsome."

They both laughed. Christmas music played in Michael's car. Darla sang along.

They arrived at Greystone's Steakhouse on Fifth Avenue in the Gaslamp Quarter.

"I didn't know a restaurant was named after me?"

"That's your surprise. This is a family-owned restaurant. It's been voted one of California's top ten steakhouses."

"Look, Michael, there's even rose petals on the tables. How romantic."

"I wanted tonight to be special."

They both ordered shrimp cocktail and the Greystone salad. Michael got the filet mignon and Darla the surf and turf. Darla could only finish her lobster.

"I'll take the steak home. I need to save room for the dessert. Did you see they have limoncello cheesecake?"

Michael laughed. While they enjoyed their dessert and coffee, Darla took a box from her purse. "Merry Christmas, Michael."

Smiling, he undid the wrapping paper and opened the box.

"Oh, Darla, this is beautiful. How did you know I've always wanted a gold cross like this. Would you put it on me, please?"

Darla got up and fastened the chain around his neck.

He gently pulled her face to his and kissed her. "Thank you."

Michael reached into his sports coat pocket and took out a small gold box.

"For you, my darling, Merry Christmas."

The box glistened from the candlelight on the table. Darla opened the box and pulled out the paper on top. It read:

Each heart represents how many months I've known you. Notice each heart gets a little bigger. The seven months we've been together, my feelings for you have grown stronger as I've gotten to know you better. Love, Michael

Oh my gosh. He's said he loves me.

Darla's hand shook as she took out the gold bracelet with seven hearts. Her mouth fell open. Her heart skipped a beat. Michael reached over and put it on her left wrist. Darla went to him—threw her arms around him. She kissed him with softness yet urgency. The warmth of her breath sent a spark of desire to Michael's senses. They both felt the electricity and intimacy of the kiss.

"Thank you, Michael. It's lovely."

Darla talked all about her time at Amy's. She showed Michael pictures of Winter Hope.

"I saw her right after she was born. What an amazing experience for me. Especially since I'm her godmother."

Darla knew she hit a soft spot. Michael suddenly looked down, obviously remembering the baby he lost.

"I guess we should get going. I'd like to sit up front tonight in church, Michael."

Michael paid the bill and helped Darla with her jacket. Taking her by the hand, he led her to his car. He was quiet on the way to church. The church service included a time of worship, communion, and a service with fellowship following.

The pastor spoke on second chances and new beginnings. Darla sat up straighter so she could listen intently to every word. She even moved to the edge of her chair. In his sermon, the pastor said you may feel weary, discouraged, or experienced loss or disappointment. He shared about having a life-giving power of hope in the face of doubt.

"In the story of Lazarus, Mary and Martha felt hopeless until their brother walked out of the tomb. They experienced a miracle not in the way or timing they expected. In Isaiah 43:18 it says: 'Do not remember the former things, or ponder the things of the past.'

"What the Bible is saying here is to stop looking behind and don't let past failures paralyze you. Look forward to new things of God. He has a fresh start for you in the new year. Anticipate that God will do something great in your life."

Thank you, God. That is exactly what I needed to hear. I am ready for a new beginning focused on you.

❧ 44 ❧

*A*fter the service, in the fellowship hall, they served coffee, tea, and eggnog. They also had assorted cookies and cakes. Darla and Michael, both full from dinner, only had eggnog. Michael was unusually quiet on the ride home, he seemed to be in deep thought. He turned to Darla when they parked at her house.

"Pastor's sermon tonight made me think about my own life—where it's going. I asked myself if I've let go of my hope. Tomorrow, can we get together and have a time of prayer?"

Darla felt a little confused. She'd never seen Michael so serious. She put her hand on his.

"Sure. Why don't you come over for breakfast around nine."

"I'll stop at the coffee shop you like and get us a cappuccino and some muffins."

They embraced. Michael slowly brought his lips to hers. His kiss was warm and inviting. She realized her love for Michael wasn't the physical lust kind. It was almost a spiritual thing—the way she admired and respected him and his love for God. Her yearning for closeness was because of his kindness and tenderness. He was someone she could trust.

Darla tossed and turned most of the night wondering about Michael's need to pray with her.

What is going on with Michael? He's usually pretty jovial. Yesterday, he was somber and deep in thought. I know it deeply affected him when I mentioned the babies.

Michael showed up at nine o'clock as promised. His mood was a little more cheerful. He hugged Darla and set down the coffee and muffins.

After they finished breakfast, Michael took hold of Darla's hands.

"Let's pray. I need some wisdom and clarification. There are some decisions I need to make. I want them to be in God's timing and part of his plan for my life."

They bowed their heads.

Michael started, "Dear Heavenly Father, we come before you today seeking your divine wisdom and guidance as we face important decisions in our lives. We acknowledge that your ways are higher than our ways. Your thoughts are higher than our thoughts. Give us clarity and lead us. Help us seek your will above all else, trusting that your plans for us are good and perfect. May we not lean on our own understanding, but acknowledge you in all our ways knowing that you will direct our paths. Provide us with godly advisors who will encourage us to make decisions that honor you. Help us to be attentive to your still small voice as we pray, study your Word, and listen to the Holy

Spirit. Give us courage to step out in faith. And peace in making decisions, knowing that you hold our future. Help us to trust in your goodness and faithfulness. May we rest in knowing that you are working all things together for our good and your glory. Guard our hearts and minds from fear, doubt, and confusion. May we not be swayed by the others' opinions or the pressures of the world. We pray we would make decisions with love and compassion, considering the impact of our choices on others. May we seek to serve and bless those around us reflecting the love and character of Jesus in all we do. Thank you, Lord, for the gift of wisdom and the promise that if we ask, you will guide our steps as we seek your face. Your wisdom will lead us in the path of righteousness and peace. We ask all this in the name of Jesus."

When Michael finished the prayer, Darla noticed her hands were wet. She looked up and saw tears on Michael's cheeks. His eyes were closed as he let the peacefulness of the moment wash over him. Michael opened his eyes and wiped them with the back of his hand.

"Let's drive to the beach and take a walk."

Darla smiled. "All right."

Neither spoke as they walked slowly on the sand. The warm sun on their skin and the sound of the waves brought a sense of calm. Michael broke the silence.

"Darla, I'm sure you're wondering why I wanted to pray specifically with you today."

Darla nodded, stopped, and looked up at him.

"It's because the decisions I need to make include you too."

Darla tilted her head to one side. One brow curled up. Her mouth opened with a perfect 'O' giving her face the look of a question mark.

"I need to be honest with you. When you were gone visiting Amy, I went to see my pastor. I guess I needed to talk to a godly man. I shared my feelings for you with him and my fear of moving forward."

Darla's eyes narrowed. She moved closer to him.

"I told him you were the most caring person I ever met, and I didn't want to let you down." Darla looked down and closed her eyes.

"A woman like Darla deserves unconditional love. I said, I don't know if I can love her like that—like I loved Rachael." Darla looked intently at Michael. She smiled warmly.

"I asked him if I was betraying Rachael's memory if I was falling in love with you. He was extremely kind and patient with me. He told me that he was an avid reader and one of his favorite author's was F. Scott Fitzgerald. You know *The Great Gatsby.*" Darla nodded.

"Well, pastor quoted him, 'There really are all kinds of love in this world, but never the same love twice.' He told me my heart may never completely heal from losing Rachael, but that I'm still capable of loving again. It won't be the same, nor would I want it to be the same. It takes great strength and courage to allow ourselves to fall in love again. That's where we have to lean on the Lord and follow where he is leading."

"He said, 'Michael, you need to pray and ask the Lord about the possibility of a new beginning.' He also shared

Romans 7:2 with me which explains that if a spouse dies the marital bond ends. That makes the surviving mate free to marry. Darla, I haven't shared my feelings like this with anyone since Rachael. I feel so close to you." Darla took him by the hand.

"Michael, let me be honest too. I have fallen in love with you. Like you, I've been scared because of what I've been through. Today when you prayed with me all that fear left. I felt God saying to me: Trust him—I want you to be with him."

Michael took her in his arms. "I felt the same peace myself during prayer. I feel as though God is sealing our relationship. Darla, I leave in a few days to attend a medical convention in New York City. It lasts for about a week. During the time I'm gone, we can both take the time separately to hear from God for our future."

Darla faced Michael. "Could we go get some coffee. I want to share something with you before you leave out of town."

At the coffee shop, Michael went up to the counter to order cappuccinos and two slices of quiche. Darla went to the restroom. While Michael was waiting for their order and for Darla to return, he noticed a magazine on one of the tables. A picture of a hot air balloon was on the cover. Darla returned and Michael picked up their order.

"What's this?" Darla asked.

"Just some magazine I picked up. I liked the cover—always wanted to ride on a hot air balloon."

"Me too," Darla said. "I think that would be so much fun."

Michael smiled and winked at Darla.

Darla touched Michael's cheek.

"I know you know about what happened in my marriage. But I never told you about the guy I followed to California and what happened with him. There is something I've never told you about my past."

Michael moved in closer.

Darla blurted out, "I had an abortion."

Michael took a slow deep breath. He didn't react, instead, he leaned over and held her in his arms.

Warm tears filled Darla's eyes. Minutes passed between them. "I can't image how hard this is for you to share with me. I'm sorry you had to experience this. I love you no matter what."

"What broke my heart was when I told the boy I was living with I was pregnant, and he excepted no responsibility. He left on a trip with his friends and let me go through the abortion by myself. I even caught him cheating on me in our house. Abortion wasn't my choice. I felt it was my only option. I lived with guilt and shame and experienced flashbacks and nightmares. Only through a relationship with God can I receive forgiveness and healing. Thank you, Michael, for not condemning me. I've kept this bottled up for years and never talked about it."

When they broke apart, Darla saw a tenderness and compassion on Michael's face that reassured her nothing changed about how he felt for her.

He is the most kindhearted, caring person I've ever known. He exemplifies the character of Jesus.

❦ 45 ❦

January 1983

During the time of Michael's absence, Darla spent a lot of time alone with God. She felt certain Michael was part of God's plan for her life. At work one afternoon, Jim Anderson called her into his office.

"Darla, you've been pretty quiet lately. Is everything okay with you and Michael? You know he's a great guy who loves the Lord. It's obvious he's crazy about you."

"Dr. Anderson, I …"

"Jim, please. This is informal."

"All right, Jim. Everything is fine with me and Michael. We've even talked about marriage."

"That's great. Then what's going on?"

"It has nothing to do with Michael. It's me. I told him something I've never told anyone about my past. I think if we are going to spend our lives together, I don't need to keep anything from him."

Dr. Anderson frowned.

Darla continued, "When I was in my early twenties, I moved in with this guy I loved and thought he loved me, until I caught him cheating on me. I found out I was pregnant. Afraid and alone, I didn't know what to do. I killed my baby. I knew it was wrong when I did it. To this day, I regret my choice. There's an intense emptiness inside me. I know God's forgiven me, but will I always live with regret."

Dr. Anderson put his hand on Darla's.

"What you did was out of fear and desperation. God gave you free will and you used it. You have to bear the consequences of your decision. God loves all his creation including your former child. Your baby will be waiting for you in heaven. All the time you may have missed together here on earth, you will spend together with your child for all eternity."

"Wow, Jim. I've never thought about it like that. Thank you. I've struggled with these questions for years about my baby—where is my baby and whether I'd ever see my baby again."

"I'm glad I could help. Please let me reassure you that telling Michael would never change his feelings for you. He loves you with the love of God."

On the way home from work, Darla stopped at the beach. She needed time to be alone with Jesus. As she sat down on the sand, the tears flowed. They were not tears of sadness, but tears of refreshing. Hugging herself tightly, she looked up toward heaven. "Thank you, Jesus, for your healing and your unconditional love. I know now you are taking care of my baby in heaven, and we'll be reunited one day."

Michael called Darla every evening just to say good night.

On one particular call, Darla told Michael, "I've been spending time alone with God. I'm removing all distractions so I can hear his voice. I've asked God to help me grow spiritually and prepare me to be a godly wife."

"Darla, I've been praying for us and for God to guide us in our relationship. I know he wants the best for us."

"Yes, Michael, we are both trusting God with our future."

"I have a surprise for you when I get home."

"A surprise? I love surprises, Michael."

"I better say good night, Darla. I'm exhausted. They kept us so busy at the convention I barely had time for lunch."

"That's okay. I just appreciate you calling. Have a great day tomorrow. I love you."

"Love you too. Good night."

Michael's plane wouldn't get into San Diego until eleven, so he told Darla not to worry about picking him up. He'd take a cab home instead.

The next day was Saturday. Darla assumed he'd be tired, so she let him rest and didn't call him.

Darla got back from walking Archie and Spanky around two o'clock when her phone rang.

"Hi, Darla." Michael's voice was brimming with joy and anticipation.

Darla's stomach fluttered, and she answered in a bubbly tone, "Welcome home, Michael. I'm excited to see you."

"Want to go get some pizza?"

"Sure. See you soon."

Darla took extra time getting ready for her dinner date with Michael. She put on a new oversized teal sweater, her favorite jeans, and some ankle boots for a casual look. Michael seemed overly excited to see her and welcomed her with opened arms. Darla's eyes sparkled. Michael took a long look at her. "You sure look cute tonight."

"Why thank you, Dr. Terry."

A huge grin seemed plastered on Michael's face.

I wonder what he's up to. He hasn't stopped grinning all through the meal.

Michael took her hand. "I have a surprise for you."

"What is it?"

"It's a surprise. All I can tell you is next Saturday I'm picking you up at two o'clock in the afternoon. Dress warm and bring a jacket."

"Are we going somewhere special?"

"No more questions. You'll have to wait until Saturday. Now, do you want a cannoli or a slice of tiramisu for dessert?"

"A cannoli, please."

All the next week, Darla was restless. She had a difficult time focusing on tasks. Her mind eagerly anticipated what would happen on Saturday. Darla felt excitement and nervousness about Michael's secret.

I wonder if he's going to propose. I'm ready to be engaged. I could spend my life with Michael.

46

Michael arrived on schedule Saturday afternoon, grinning from ear to ear. After he sat Darla in the car, he pulled out a blindfold.

"I need to blindfold you, so you won't know where we are going."

Darla couldn't sit still. Butterflies danced in her stomach with anticipation of what was next.

What is Michael up to? Why is he blindfolding me? Michael stopped the car. He went around and opened her door. He took her by the arm. They walked for what seemed like a long time. With every step, Darla grew more excited. Michael removed the blindfold. Right there in front of them was the hot air balloon.

"Surprise!" Michael threw his hands up.

Darla's mouth fell open. She clapped her hands together and danced a little jig.

"Michael, this is awesome! You remembered what I told you at the coffee shop. I've always wanted to ride in a hot air balloon. What a magical adventure."

They got into the ballon. It soared high in the air.

"Darla, quick, look down."

Looking over the side of the ballon, she watched as the workers on the ground unfolded a banner.

Darla's heart stopped. Her eyes and mouth flew open wide with excitement.

"Oh my." The banner read: *Will You Marry Me?*

Darla jumped into Michael's arms screaming, "Yes! Yes!"

He raised her face to his, running his fingers through her hair. He kissed her. His kiss held tenderness, passion, joy, and promise. They had a road to travel, doing life together.

This moment. This dream. Thank you, Lord, for bringing this wonderful man into my life.

They both started to laugh uncontrollably. Darla wondered if it was the altitude or the excitement of the moment. Holding on to Michael, Darla pointed. "Look at the amazing colors cast by the sun setting over the ocean."

"It's beautiful. But not as beautiful as your smile—it's like a ray of sunshine to me."

Michael got down on one knee. "I want to spend the rest of my life cherishing and loving you."

He took out the ring and placed it on her finger. Remarkably, it fit perfectly. When the balloon touched down, Darla once again was astonished by the amazing spread waiting for them.

There on the hillside, the balloon crew set out tables with white linen tablecloths. Arrayed on the tables were vases with red roses and baby breath. They served the couple the Louis Roederer Champagne in gold-rimmed glasses. White porcelain plates held salted almonds, mini quiches, canapés, and crab rangoons. When Darla and Michael finished snacking, the crew packed up the remaining food in gold and white charcuterie boxes for them to take home along with the rest of the champagne. They handed Darla a decorative basket that contained the two gold-rimmed champagne glasses, the *Will You Marry Me* banner, and the complimentary photo.

"Congratulations," echoed the balloon crew as Michael and Darla walked to his car.

"Michael, thank you for a wonderful romantic sunset balloon ride. What a way to propose."

"We have the banner and photo to remember this day always. What are you going to do the banner?"

"I think I'll hang it up in my living room. Then everyone who comes in sees it. You know what I'd really like right now?"

"What would you like right now, my love?"

"A slice of red velvet cake and a cup of coffee."

"I know just the place. Let's go pick up the cake and go back to your place. You can make some coffee."

"I think that's a good idea. I'm sure Spanky and Archie are wondering where we are."

They picked up two red velvet cupcakes and two carrot cake cupcakes. Darla made coffee while Michael took the dogs out. When he returned, he hung up the banner for her.

As they enjoyed their dessert, Michael asked, "How about getting married on February thirteen? I don't want to wait."

"I think it would be a good day to get married. Let's just have a small wedding—family and close friends."

"Yes. Small will work. I plan on talking to my parents tomorrow. You know they're medical missionaries in Botswana. I want to make sure they can come home for the wedding before we set the date."

"Okay."

"It's getting late. I guess I better go, so we can both get up for church."

"See you in the morning."

Michael kissed her long and hard. Then he turned to leave. "I love you."

"Love you too."

Darla fell into bed exhausted from the excitement of the day. She really wanted to phone Amy or Rayleen with the wonderful news but decided it was too late. Darla drifted into a heavy sleep.

The ring of her phone woke her.

"Good morning."

"Good morning, Michael."

"Are you still in bed?"

"Yes. I fell asleep and forgot to set my alarm."

"How about we go to the second service, then you won't have to rush."

Darla breathed a sigh of relief. She hated to be pushed for time. Just as she finished the last touches of her makeup, the phone rang.

"Hello."

"Darla, hi, it's Amy. I didn't think you'd be home. I

thought you'd still be at church. I was just going to leave you a message."

"I overslept. We are going to the second service."

"I don't want to keep you. It's just you've been on my heart the last few days."

"I'm glad you called. I was going to call you this afternoon. I have some exciting news."

"You do? What is it?"

"Michael proposed yesterday."

"Yippee! I'm so happy for you."

Just then the doorbell rang. "I've got to go, Amy. I'll call you later. Michael's here to take me to church."

After church, Michael came over for lunch. Darla made tuna melt sandwiches. Michael played with the dogs.

When they finally sat down to eat, Michael said, "I have good news."

"You do?"

"Yes. My parents will be able to make it home for our wedding."

"That's great. Now we can solidify our plans. I have an idea for a venue for the ceremony and reception."

"Yes."

"Actually, when I accompanied Rayleen on her search for her wedding venue, we looked at the Mission Bay Resort. I liked it there. That could be a possibility for us."

"Would you like to take a ride out there and check it out today?"

"Sure. Let's go."

47

On the drive out to Mission Bay, Michael said, "I don't think we will have more than thirty or forty people at the wedding."

"I counted our family, friends, and co-workers. If they all show up, it will be thirty-four people."

When they arrived at the resort, the guide, Mr. Gibson, greeted them. "Can you tell me a little about your wedding plans?"

Michael looked at Darla.

"You go ahead and tell him what we talked about."

"Well, it's going to be a small wedding—less than fifty people."

"I'll take you around to our different wedding settings. You two can decide on the one you like."

The guide took them to indoor and outdoor settings. They arrived at the grassy area with the beach in the background. Michael and Darla smiled at each other.

"This is it. Look at the tropical gardens, the unobstructed view of the ocean with sailboats going by. There's even palm fronds on each side of the area where we would exchange out vows."

"Wow, you're right. What great pictures this would make."

Mr. Gibson said, "This is one of our most preferred settings. The weather should still be good in February. You could host your reception right here on the patio. You'd be dining under the stars. The sunsets here are incredible. Our package includes the white garden folding chairs, the wedding singers, the sound system, the plated dinner, and d'oeuvres."

"Mr. Gibson, we would like a champagne toast—no open bar. We'll be bringing our own pastor to officiate the wedding."

"Sounds good. Also, part of our package you will receive a discounted overnight accommodation for you and your guests."

Michael and Mr. Gibson sat down so he could give him a quote for under fifty people. They shook hands. Michael gave him a deposit and booked the date—Saturday, February thirteenth.

"I'll get back to you within the week to let you know if there are any others who would like to take advantage of the overnight stay. Darla and I will stay the night after our reception. Then fly out the next morning for our honeymoon."

When they got back to Darla's place, he told her to sit down.

"Darla, there's one more thing we need to decide on. What do you think about going to Cabo San Lucas for our honeymoon?"

"That sounds like a great idea. Is that far from Pastor Sepulveda's orphanage?"

"Not too far. I knew you'd ask that. I already thought about it. It's one of the reasons I chose Mexico. How would you like to make a stop at the orphanage on the way home?"

Darla pumped her fist in the air. "Hallelujah!"

"By the way," Michael said. "My parents will be staying at my house when they come for our wedding. They've planned an extended week's vacation while we're on our honeymoon."

"That's great. My parents are staying for an extra week at my house. Maybe they can get together."

"Aren't Amy and Steve staying at the resort?"

"Yes, Michael. They want to hang out with Rayleen and Clayton who'll be staying at Mission Bay too."

The following week, Darla took her friend shopping with her to find a dress for the wedding. "I am not going to get a traditional white dress. I've already done that. This time, Rayleen, my dress will be colorful."

"Okay. Let's shop."

At the third store they entered, Darla spotted the dress.

"That's it. Rayleen, look."

"Wow. Talk about color—that cobalt blue sure is vibrant. Hurry, try it on."

When Darla exited the dressing room, Rayleen and the salesgirl both gasped.

The salesgirl spoke first. "I've seen several other women

try on that dress. None of them wear it like you. It's striking with your hair color and figure."

"She's right. Darla, I can't think of the word that truly describes you in that dress. I know—dramatic. The gleaming rhinestone starburst pin on the waist enhances the entire look of the dress."

"I'll take it. We should look for a tie in the same color for Michael to wear with the white jacket he's wearing for the wedding."

They found the exact color tie they needed. Darla picked up a pair of flat silver shoes to go with her dress. Rayleen suggested she'd be more comfortable wearing flats all day.

Darla got home and found Michael at the front door grinning like a Cheshire Cat.

"Hi, Michael."

"Hey, Darla. I couldn't wait to tell you the news."

"Tell me what?"

"I was able to book the Four Seasons Resort in Cabo San Lucas for the week of our honeymoon. We have an ocean front suite. It comes complete with a plunge pool."

Darla's cheeks flushed a rosy pink from the excitement bubbling within her. A wide smile spread across her face. No words could express her happiness. She threw her arms around his neck.

"So glad you're delighted with our honeymoon destination. I have one more surprise for you."

"You do? What?"

"Well, you know how we talked about selling our homes to be able to pick out something together."

"Yes. I remember. But we decided to put it on hold until after our wedding."

"You're right. Something has come up. One of the doctors in my building told me he is retiring. He's planning on selling his home and moving closer to his family in Arizona. His house is perfect for us. It's in La Jolla Farms, and the property has a beautiful view of the Pacific Ocean. He said he would sell it with a contingency that we sell our homes, and he finds the house he wants. Would you like to go see it before he hires a real estate agent?"

"Sure. When?"

"We could go right now."

"Let's go."

When she set foot in the doctor's house, Darla's eyes grew wide. It was like walking into a dream. The kitchen and living room had large windows looking out at the ocean. The floors were covered with Brazilian cherry hardwood. The master bedroom had a window seat and a separate vanity suite.

"What do you think?" Michael asked.

"I love it, Michael. Do we need four bedrooms?"

"We might. You never know what plans God has for our family."

"The price is fair. I'm going to put an offer on it and leave the rest up to God."

Darla smiled. She gave Michael a big hug.

48

Over the next several days, Michael and Darla busily planned for their wedding. Together they shopped for gifts for the wedding party and for their wedding bands. She found personalized bridesmaid robes for Amy and Rayleen in pink and got a white one for herself. Michael took her to a specialized gift store where they found personalized leather toiletry bags for the two groomsmen. At the jewelry store, they decided on plain gold wedding bands with specks of diamonds in them.

Michael's parents arrived three weeks before the wedding day. Michael and Darla picked them up at San Diego International Airport. The four of them went to dinner at the Bencotto Restaurant in Little Italy.

Dale Terry, Michael's father, was over six feet with thick brown eyebrows and brown eyes gleaming like polished chestnuts. His brown hair was sprinkled with gray at the temple. He was mild-mannered and polite.

Michael's mother, Christine, was short with a cute blond

bob hairstyle. She had sapphire blue eyes with a captivating smile. She hugged Darla.

"It's an honor to meet you, Christine and Dale," Darla said.

"We are so glad to meet the woman who made my son so happy. It's obvious, he's crazy about you."

"Thank you, Christine."

Dale looked over at Michael. "This food is delicious. Italian food is one of the things we missed most living in Africa. This is a real treat for us, son."

"I'm glad you enjoyed it, Dad. I guess I need to get you both home. I'm sure you're exhausted after flying all day."

"Yes. We'll probably sleep all day tomorrow while you're at work."

Darla instantly fell in love with Michael's parents. It was refreshing to be around genuine people. She could tell their feelings were sincere.

To help Darla out while she was at work, Rayleen picked Darla's parents up from the airport.

When Darla arrived home that evening, her mom had an amazing dinner of tri-tip steak awaiting her. Michael joined them for dinner. He was an instant hit with her parents.

Darla's mom remarked about Michael's smile. "That man has the cutest smile. It seems to be perpetually frozen on his face. He sure loves you. I watch the way he gloats over you."

Darla blushed.

Dale Terry and Darla's dad connected immediately—both in the medical profession.

Amy and Steven flew in from New York on Friday

morning. They rented a car at the airport and went right to the Mission Bay Resort. She called Darla a little after noon, knowing she'd only be working a half day.

"Hi, Darla."

"Hi, Amy. How was your flight?"

"The flight was good. We are at the resort. This place is amazing. They put a basket on our bedspread with fruit, chocolates, and a bottle of sparkling cider. Your wedding will be lovely here."

"Thanks. I think so too. I'll see you in the morning. Remember, the hairdresser will be there at nine o'clock. My dad will take you to the airport when you leave. He's using my car while we're gone."

Michael picked Darla up early Saturday morning, so they could stop for breakfast.

"Michael, I think I only want some coffee and a muffin."

"Are you nervous?"

"No. Not at all, Michael. I just know there's going to be a lot of food at the reception. Actually, I'm pretty calm."

"It's God's peace, Darla. You're in his perfect will."

"I know you're right. God brought you into my life." Darla's eyes softened, with a subtle tilt of her head she gazed at Michael with a gentle, warm smile.

Mr. Gibson was right there to greet them when they pulled into the valet parking at the resort. Before he took them to their room, he wanted them to check on the setup for their wedding tomorrow to be sure they were satisfied. They immediately noticed white satin ribbons on the backs of the garden folding chairs.

"Look at that, Michael. They put a wedding arbor for us to stand under while we exchange our vows."

"Yes. Look, it's decorated with beautiful roses and carnations along with the greenery. Even the flower centerpieces on the tables totally compliment the arbor flowers."

"The white rose petals line the aisle where you'll be walking. It will be the epitome of excellence," Mr. Gibson chimed in.

"It's all perfect. Thank you."

When they arrived at their room, they not only found the same goodies Amy and Steven found, but white rose petals were sprinkled on top of the lavender bed spread. The room phone rang.

"Hi. Miss Greystone. We want to let you know your hair stylist is here."

"Thank you. Can you send her up to the bridal suite."

"All right, Miss Greystone. I've already phoned your friend Amy. She's on her way up too."

Darla turned to Michael. "Hurry, Michael. Amy and Rayleen are on their way up to get ready. You and the groomsmen are all getting ready in Clayton's room."

"Okay. See you at our wedding." They both laughed and hugged.

A few minutes later, a knock sounded at the door. Darla opened it to find Rayleen and Amy standing there holding their bridesmaid dresses and a small makeup tote. The girls jumped up and down laughing and singing, "You're getting married today."

Before Darla could invite them in, Lisa, the hair stylist, walked up. "Hi, ladies. Ready to get gorgeous."

"Yes," they echoed together.

It took several hours for the women to get ready. All three of them chose to have their hair down.

Lisa did a great job of entwining artificial baby breath in Darla's hair along with rhinestone hair clips to match the pin on her dress. Amy found matching rhinestone barrettes for her and Rayleen to wear. Mr. Gibson sent up a complimentary cheese and cracker plate with cold drinks for them to snack on.

49

February 1983

At ten minutes to four, the three of them hurried down to stay in the waiting area until everyone was seated. The wedding march played. Darla's father took her arm and walked her to the front.

The pastor spoke, "Who gives this woman to be married?"

Darla's father answered, "I do."

Michael moved over next to Darla. Before he faced the pastor, he looked deep into her eyes and mouthed the words, "I love you."

She smiled and whispered, "I love you too."

Lord thank you. I know this will be a forever marriage because you are the center of it.

The wedding singer sang "I Will Be There." Darla held back happy tears.

The pastor began, "There are some things Michael and

Darla want to say to one another before they take their vows."

The couple faced one another. Michael took both of Darla's hands in his. "Darla, I want you to know, I promise to guide and protect you as Christ does his church as long as we live. God's word gives us the perfect example of this love in Christ's death. I shall always try, with God's help, to show you this same kind of love, for I know that in his sight we are both one."

"Michael, I thank God for you. I thank him for second chances. I promise to stand by you, support you, and be your forever helpmate."

They turned around still holding hands and faced the pastor. He led them through the exchange of vows.

"You may now kiss your bride."

Michael and Darla embraced with bright smiles on their faces. They headed to the receiving line. Instead of throwing rice, the guests threw white rose petals.

Michael grabbed Darla to dance their first dance as husband and wife. The wedding singer sang "I Can't Help Falling In Love."

Next, Darla's father danced with her to the song "Father And Daughter." Once the wedding party was seated, Michael's father gave a champagne toast.

Amy stood up and said, "Darla is my best friend. I don't know a better man for her than Michael. I wish them many, many years of happiness."

Michael's father came over to Darla. "Would you do me the honor and dance with me?"

"It would be my pleasure."

"I want to thank you for coming into my son's life and making him so happy."

"He makes me happy too, Dr. Terry."

"Dad, please."

"His mother and I didn't know if he'd ever get over losing his wife. They were so in love. To lose her like that devastated him. I thank God for giving him another love, someone special like you."

"Thank you, Dad."

The photographer shot amazing photos of Darla and Michael's wedding. The sunset backdrop created incredible colors for the pictures. He was able to also get a silhouette of the couple. Since they weren't flying out for their honeymoon until eleven o'clock the next day, they stayed at their reception.

Rayleen walked up to Darla. "This is the most fun wedding reception I've ever been at. Michael's parents have danced to almost every song."

"I know they are having a good time. They've really clicked with my parents."

At 10:00 p.m., Darla told Michael, "I'm tired and everyone is getting ready to leave."

"Okay. Let me just remind my mom to bring our gifts home."

When they went up to their room, Michael took Darla in his arms. "You have made me the happiest man tonight."

"And you, Michael, have blessed my life."

Their wedding night was filled with intimacy and shared joy. The essence of the night was about celebrating their love and commitment to one another and starting a new chapter in their lives.

The next morning, Michael woke up smothered in kisses.

"Wake up, Dr. Terry."

"Mrs. Terry, that sounds amazing."

Darla fell into Michael's arms. The alarm went off.

"Oh no. Things were just getting good."

"Listen, husband, we have the rest of our lives for this. We need to hurry and get ready for the airport."

"You're right, Darla. You go ahead and shower first. You probably need more time to get ready."

While Darla got ready, Michael ordered room service for breakfast. They were already packed for their honeymoon. As soon as they finished eating, the shuttle took them to the airport. On the plane, Michael told the flight attendant they were on their honeymoon.

"Congratulations you two." She handed them a complimentary bottle of champagne.

❧ 50 ❧

When they arrived at San Jose de Cabo International Airport, the rental car Michael had arranged was waiting for them. The Four Seasons Resort was something out of a dream.

"Look at this room, Michael. It speaks luxury. There's a breathtaking view from every angle of our balcony."

"Come on, Darla. We have our own private plunge pool. Hurry, go get ready."

Darla quickly changed into her two-piece bathing suit. She turned and spotted his swim trunks still lying on the bed. Already self-conscience because he'd never seen her in a swimsuit, now she was even more nervous as she walked toward the pool. Michael began laughing.

"Darla, it's our pool. No one else is here. You didn't need to wear a swimsuit. We're married, remember?"

Darla splashed him and jumped in. He came right over to her. He pulled her against him. Their lips clung together softly, then with more urgency. She whispered his name and felt his smile. He tasted like all she loved—chocolate, caramel, and strawberries. Tenderly, he lifted her out of the pool. He carried her to their bed. With one arm wrapped tightly around her waist, he pulled her close to his chest. Gently running his fingers through her hair, down her back, and taking in every inch of her. Darla looked up at him, her eyes full of adoration. She was totally vulnerable to him opening her body and mind to him.

Darla wasn't sure at what point they fell asleep, but when she awoke to butterfly kisses, it already was dark.

"Well, my wife, you wore me out. I don't know about you, but I'm famished."

"I'm hungry too, Michael." Downstairs they found the Palmerio Restaurant. It was featured as a Mediterranean love letter to the Baja Riviera. They dined outside on the patio by candlelight surrounded by stunning moonlight.

"I couldn't have asked for a more romantic dinner, Michael. The presentation of the food is as amazing as the food."

"You're right, Darla. This Chenin Blanc wine definitely compliments the snapper."

"What should we order for dessert, Michael?"

"Let's try the mint chocolate chip gelato."

After they finished their meal, they went back to their room. Together they snuggled on the coach, looking out at a sea of stars.

I feel so safe in Michael's arms—emotionally connected and supported.

"What are you thinking about, my love?"

"Us and the many experiences we have to look forward to as husband and wife."

During the next few days, they explored the Cabo San

Lucas Arch on an exciting snorkeling coastal tour. Next, they were off to the charming colonial town of Todos Santos. There they visited the mission of Our Lady Del Pilar. They experienced the allure of the iconic Hotel California learning it was constructed in 1947. The following day, the couple rode horseback along the beach. They topped off the last day of their honeymoon on a luxury yacht. Dinner was served by a renowned chef. Darla marveled at the spectacular colorful sunset from the deck of the yacht.

Although they enjoyed an incredible time in Cabo, Darla anxiously awaited going to visit Maria at the orphanage. Maria had been foremost in her mind during their honeymoon. The next morning, they prepared to leave the resort and drive to the orphanage.

Darla walked out of the shower—Michael stood up with a mischievous grin on his face.

"Well, my husband, why are you grinning like that?"

"I just got some great news. I talked with my dad while you were showering. He told me the doctor whose house we put an offer on, accepted our offer. He found a house, and he put an offer on it. We also received two offers for your house and one for mine. It looks like we'll be able to get that house."

"Wow, all that happened so quick. It must be part of God's plan for us."

"Yes. But there's more. Now that we're going to have this big house, we have to fill up the rooms."

"What do you mean?"

"How would you like to take a little girl home with us?"

"You mean Maria?" Her mouth quivered with the thrill of the moment. She jumped into Michael's arms.

"Yes, my darling. I've talked to Pastor Sepulveda, and because Maria has no living relatives that can be located, adopting her would be simple. I've already hired an International adoption attorney to help us through the process.

Darla's heart raced. A wave of pure joy washed over her. She couldn't help shedding tears of happiness.

"Michael, Maria loves you too. I know we can be good parents to her. God has blessed us beyond anything I could ever image. Come on. Let's get on our knees and thank him."

"Yes. Let's do that."

Michael and Darla knelt side by side next to the couch. He took her hands, and they bowed their heads.

Michael began the prayer. "Dear Heavenly Father, we thank you so much for the gift of Maria you are blessing us with. We promise to raise her to know and love you. Help us to always keep you first in our lives. In Jesus's name, Amen."

Darla had a hard time sitting still in the car on the way to the orphanage. The drive was breathtaking. Michael kept pointing things out to distract her. She enjoyed the view, but she couldn't hide the spark of excitement in her eyes.

Pastor Sepulveda and Belinda greeted them when they arrived.

"I didn't mention to the children you were coming. I wanted it to be a surprise."

Belinda went to get Maria, Lucinda, José, and Enrique. Michael left to get the gifts they brought for the children out of the car. When the children spotted Darla and Michael, they raced into their arms.

"Miss Darla, Dr. Terry, you are here. I prayed we'd see you again," Maria shouted.

They all sat down at the picnic tables to pass out the gifts. Radiant smiles spread across their faces as they opened their treasures.

Only Maria hesitated. She held on to Darla.

"I love you, Miss Darla. I missed you so much."

As she held Darla's hand, she lifted it up.

"What's this?"

She pointed to Darla's ring. She leaned over to Michael lifting his hand up as well.

"You have a ring too. Are you two..?"

Michael interrupted her, "Yes, Maria. We are married."

Maria stood, suddenly seemingly deep in thought. She touched her temple.

"Then you can be parents." A bright grin spread across her face.

Just then Pastor Sepulveda came out and announced, "Miss Belinda needs you children to come help her in the kitchen. Darla and Michael are going to join us for dinner."

The children hurried and picked up their things, following him to the kitchen. Only Maria kept looking back.

Darla and Michael put their suitcases in the room they would be staying in for the night. Then they dressed for dinner. After dinner, Pastor Sepulveda motioned them to his office while Belinda had the children get washed up for bed.

Pastor Sepulveda sat down at his desk. He picked up a folder and opened it.

"Have a seat you two. I've made all the legal arrangements for you to adopt Maria here in Mexico. The attorney you hired, Michael, says he can make it go as quickly and smoothy as possible for you to bring her into the United States. Since he specializes in both international adoption and US immigration, he thinks you may only have to wait for about two months to bring her home."

Darla and Michael looked at each other.

We would love for you to stay a day or two after we share the news with Maria tomorrow. I think it would help her adjust to the transition better."

"We want to do whatever is best for Maria," Michael replied. Darla nodded her head in agreement.

"Let's wait and tell Maria in the morning. I think if we tell her tonight, she'll be too excited to sleep." Darla tossed and turned all night, waking Michael several times.

"What's wrong? Why are you so restless?"

"I know Maria loves us. But what if she really doesn't want to leave her friends, Belinda and Tom, or Mexico. This is her home. This is all she's ever known."

"Relax and trust God. There are no 'what ifs' when God is in control. He hasn't led us this far to let us down."

"You're right. Good night, my love."

Right after breakfast, Pastor Sepulveda, Belinda, Michael, Darla, and Maria gathered in the pastor's office. Maria fidgeted in her chair, afraid she may be in trouble.

Pastor Sepulveda spoke first, "Maria, you know Belinda and I love you just like we love our own children. Since we have our own family, sometimes we can't give you all the attention you need. How would you like to have your own family?"

Surprise stole the air from her lungs leaving Maria breathless. Her mouth seemed clamped shut.

She was stunned into silence.

Pastor continued, "Maria, I need you to make a decision. Doctor and Mrs. Terry have asked to become your parents."

"They want me to be their little girl?" Maria asked, her voice shaking.

"Yes, Maria. We love you and want you to be part of our family."

Maria threw her arms around Darla's neck.

"Yes. Miss Darla. I'll be your daughter." Her eyes widened. "Can I call you Mommy and Daddy?"

Michael moved in and took her by the hands. "Of course. We would love that."

Maria stated laughing and singing, "Mommy! Daddy! Mommy, Daddy!"

∽ 51 ∽

May 1983

A little over two months later, Darla and Michael's international adoption was finalized. Maria was legally cleared in Mexico for adoption by US citizens. As soon as their plane touched down in Mexico, Darla and Michael hurried to the orphanage. Belinda had Maria all packed and ready to leave the next morning. That night, the adults along with the children enjoyed a wonderful dinner together. Later, they sang praise songs as they roasted marshmallows around a campfire.

The next morning, Lucinda, José, and Enrique were there to say goodbye. The children were so happy for Maria. Only Lucinda shed a tear. Michael promised they'd come back next year for a visit.

A few weeks after they arrived home, Darla's parents threw a welcome home party for Maria. Michael's parents were able to return to the states to be part of the celebration.

Rayleen and Clayton brought their little girl Winter with them. Maria loved playing with the baby. Amy and Steven promised to come visit next year.

Darla and Michael happily moved Maria into their new home. Maria loved the pink bedroom. She placed all her stuffed animals on the window seat. Spanky and Archie spent more time in Maria's room now.

One night at dinner, Michael noticed how tired and worn out Darla looked. "Darla, I think you're wearing yourself out. We have the rest of our lives to fix up this house. You're taking on too much. You have your job all day, taking care of Maria, and working on the house at night."

"I'm just a little tired."

"No. I think you may be coming down with something or you could be low on iron. I'm going to take you in this week to see Dr. Elliot. She's a woman doctor in my building. Let me know which day you can get the afternoon off."

Two days later, Michael drove Darla to the doctor. Dr. Elliot was an attractive woman, tall with shoulder length blonde hair and espresso brown eyes. She looked more like a television commercial doctor than a practicing physician. She examined Darla and did some lab work.

Michael and Darla waited patiently for the doctor to discuss the test results.

The nurse came out. "Dr. Elliot will see you now."

Michael took Darla by the hand. They went into the office and sat down.

"So, doctor is Darla all right?"

"Well, Michael, she's definitely low on iron and will need to get on a stronger regimen of vitamins because of her condition."

"Her condition? What's wrong with her? What does she have?"

"She's going to be a mother."

Darla gasped. She grabbed Michael's arm. Michael jumped up.

"A baby!"

He pulled Darla up and spun her around and shouted, "We're going to have a baby."

Dr. Elliot laughed.

"You need to take your wife home. She needs to take it easy and rest. She is fatigued and has a mild form of anemia. It is due to her low iron level. It can be normal during the first trimester of pregnancy because of increased blood volume. The prenatal vitamins I prescribed will provide her with more iron, B12, and folic acid. Make sure she eats foods high in iron like spinach, lean beef, and turkey. I want her to stay on the prenatal vitamins and iron supplements."

Dr. Elliot continued, "In three weeks, you need to go see Dr. Berry. He's an obstetrician in the building next door. He's one of the best OB/GYN doctors I know. He will further evaluate you and do a sonogram to determine the sex of your baby."

Michael followed the doctor's orders. He made sure Darla took it easy the next few weeks. He hired a housekeeper to help out and do some cooking.

The day of her visit with Dr. Berry, Michael took the day off to accompany her to the appointment. Darla sat quietly in the waiting room filling out the pre-visit questionnaire. One of the questions bothered her—any previous pregnancies. She did not want to lie, so she listed the abortion. Dr. Berry was a big man with a thick Texas accent. He looked like he'd be right at home in a ten gallon hat. The doctor shook their hands with a big friendly smile.

"So, you all are going to have a baby. Today we will find out if you need to buy trucks or dolls." He laughed heartily. "I'm going to run some tests to see if the anemia has decreased and do a pelvic exam. Then we'll do the sonogram."

After Dr. Berry finished examining Darla, the nurse prepared her for the sonogram. Dr. Berry smeared some goo over her belly then ran a transducer over it. Chuckling out loud, he looked up at Michael. "Get ready to have a tea party with your little girl. After you get dressed, Darla, I'd like to meet with you both in my office."

"Okay."

Michael and Darla looked at one another. Confusion on their faces.

Could something be wrong with the baby?

Once they were seated in Dr. Berry's office, he began, "First, I want to congratulate you on the little girl you're bringing into this world. What I am going to share next I'm sorry if it causes any unpleasantness."

Darla took a deep breath.

Dr. Berry continued, "I need you to be fully aware of the risks involved. A woman who had had an abortion often can have a difficult time carrying her baby to full term. My recommendation is to put you on partial bed rest. That doesn't mean you stay in bed all day. You will be allowed some sitting, standing, and walking. I want to make certain the anemia is under control. We are doing all we can to assure you have a healthy baby girl."

Michael and Darla decided she would take a pregnancy leave of absence from her job. Darla cherished the extra time with Maria. Her daughter was thrilled to have her mother around more.

Michael hired an interior decorator to help finish with the remodeling of the home. Michael brought Darla the cutest pregnancy clothes.

"Why do you keep buying me all these clothes. I'm only going to be pregnant for a few more months?"

"I want my wife to be stylish. You are the prettiest pregnant lady I know."

Darla laughed and hugged his neck. As time progressed, the anemia cleared up, and Darla's iron levels were perfect. She no longer looked tired but instead, had a rosy glow to her cheeks.

At her OB appointment, Dr. Berry said, "Everything looks good. Your little girl's growing fine. It won't be long now."

He looked over at Michael. "You need to pack her overnight bag and get ready to be a father."

Michael smiled. "Yes, Dr. Berry. I'm so ready."

Darla's parents came from New York to stay with her and Michael. They knew she would need help with Maria.

❧ 52 ❧

November 1983

Late one afternoon, her parents left to do some shopping at the grocery store. Darla stood in the kitchen chopping vegetables for a salad, while Maria sat at the table coloring.

All of a sudden, Maria screamed, "Mommy, you're leaking."

Darla looked down to see she was standing in a puddle of water.

"Oh my, Maria, call Daddy. The baby's coming!"

Michael arrived at the house, just as Darla's parents were pulling up.

"What's wrong, Michael? Why are you home?"

"Baby's coming. Going to take Darla to the hospital," he shouted, as he ran in the front door.

"Darla, I'm here."

"I'm ready to go."

Darla's dad carried in the groceries. He said, "We'll take Maria and meet you at the hospital."

Dr. Berry was there at the hospital waiting for them. He examined Darla. "Baby's on the way."

Michael held Darla's hand when the pains began. Her labor lasted only three hours. Michael was there every step of the way.

All of sudden, Dr. Berry yelled, "Push. Here she comes."

Warm tears of joy spilled down Michael's cheeks. He whispered a silent prayer thanking God for a healthy baby and healthy wife. Darla knew he was thinking about his wife and baby he lost during delivery.

Darla broke into his thoughts, "Look at her, Michael. She's perfect."

The nurse laid the baby on her breast. Darla giggled because her little girl latched right on. "Isn't she beautiful? She's our little Lani Joy."

They had chosen the name Lani after Michael's grandmother. Joy because of the joy she brought into their lives. Michael leaned over and kissed Darla. Then he kissed Lani on top of her head and said, "She must be finished nursing. Look, she's fallen asleep."

Darla's parents and Maria filed into the room.

"Congratulations, Darla. She sure is beautiful. You've made me a grandfather."

"So precious and now I'm a grandmother. Maria, that's your baby sister."

"Wow, Mommy. Am I really a big sister now?"

Everyone laughed.

"Yes, Maria. You are the big sister. Come meet Lani Joy."

"Well, we all need to leave and let Darla get some rest, so I can bring her home tomorrow."

Darla looked up at her loving family.

I am so blessed.

After everyone left, the nurse laid Lani Joy in the small crib beside the bed. Darla took a long look at her daughter. Her heart felt as if it would burst. Gazing upward, she raised her hands in praise.

"Thank you, Lord, for this precious child you've given me. Thank you for my loving husband. For my supportive family and friends. But most of all, I am grateful for knowing you. Not only did you save me and give me a second chance, you loved me so much that you sent your son to die on the cross in my place and take the punishment I deserved for my sins. When Jesus came into my life, he turned it around full circle. He took away all my mistakes, all my pain, and all my brokenness. He made me a child of God. I love you, Jesus, with all my heart. Thank you—because of you—heartbreak is not my home—anymore."

A NOTE FROM THE AUTHOR

Dear Reader,

I wrote this book to be an encouragement for you. We all know what it's like to have a broken heart. When you've been bruised by life it's easy to get stuck in your pain. But God is ready to walk right into your circumstances and heal the broken pieces of your life once you open your heart to him. Don't let your circumstances define you. Remind yourself what God says about you—he loves you with an everlasting love, you are precious in his sight and you are a child of God. He created you for a unique purpose and adopted you into his family.

Remember you are not alone in your brokenness. Psalm 34:18 says: *The Lord is close to the brokenhearted and saves those who have a crushed spirit.* God will take what is broken in your life and make it into something beautiful. Put your faith today in the God of hope and new beginnings.

I love hearing from you and can't wait to hear what you think of the story.

Blessings,

Dejah

dejah05@gmail.com
www.deeplylovedbyHim.com

DISCUSSION QUESTIONS

1. Darla's rebellion seemed from her relationship issues with her parents. What was the root of it?

2. When Darla found out she was pregnant what kept her from returning home? How might her life been different if she had done that?

3. When Darla learns of Giani's deceit she hires a private investigator. Do you think she did the right thing instead of confronting Giani? Why do you think she confronted his wife Sophia?

4. The sexual assault Travis endured caused him to live a lie. How did God turn this around for good?

5. Darla's life changes when she encounters Christ. How were you personally convinced of Christ's love for you? What led to that moment, and how did it affect your life?

6. How if at all, did this book relate to your own life?

7. Discuss the believability of the characters and their reactions to situations.

8. How did the book's ending make you feel? What message did it leave you with?